Father
and Son

Father and Son

DARRELL SIFFORD

Bridgebooks
Philadelphia

Book Design by Alice Derr

First edition

Bridgebooks
Published by The Westminster Press⁎
Philadelphia, Pennsylvania

PRINTED IN THE UNITED STATES OF AMERICA
9 8 7 6 5 4 3 2 1

Library of Congress Cataloging in Publication Data

Sifford, Darrell, 1931–
    Father and son.

    "Bridgebooks."
    1. Sifford, Darrell, 1931–   . 2. Divorced fathers—
United States—Biography. 3. Divorced fathers—United
States—Family relationships. 4. Fathers and sons.
I. Title.
HQ756.S536 1982   306.8′9′0924   82-11063
ISBN 0-664-27004-2

To Jay and Grant,
whose tickets, like mine, have been punched

Contents

Acknowledgments

This book would not have been possible without the help and encouragement of many persons who not only contributed to the content and form of the final manuscript but who also made less lonely and frightening my excursion into the yesteryears of my life.

I especially want to thank Laura Hobe, the editor who suggested that I write this book and whose guidance helped keep it on track; Bob McIntyre, who consistently has been a source of support; my wife, Marilyn, who makes everything possible; Jay and Grant, my sons, who have survived adversity and who seem stronger because of it.

I am also deeply appreciative of the many mental health professionals and friends whose insights have been so invaluable to me over the years and from whom I have extracted so much that ultimately became part of my life philosophy.

Prologue

This is a story about what happened to me and my two sons in the aftermath of my separation and divorce from their mother, who was my wife for almost twenty-two years.

It's a story of fear, pain, and defeat; of courage, joy, and ultimately, victory. But it's more than a story about the three of us. It could be the story of any American family that finds itself blown by the whirlwinds of discontent and disillusionment and that then undertakes the exquisite agony of picking up the pieces after the explosion. It could be your story.

As a newspaper columnist, I often write about the dynamics of family relationships, including my own. The glimpses that I reveal into my past come, not because I am an emotional exhibitionist, which I'm not, but because I believe that it can be helpful for some of those who are struggling to find that others have fought the same battles and, to varying degrees, have survived.

I'm accustomed to opening myself as a writer, yet when I was approached about the possibility of writing this book on parent-child reconciliation after divorce, I was both hesitant and frightened.

11

Why? Because I knew that it would be the most difficult, most draining piece of writing that I had ever done. I not only would have to go back and relive the grief and turmoil but I also would have to reexperience the feelings, cry the tears, suffer through the nightmares of blinding terror that more than once rocked me from sleep with screams of "Oh, no, no!"

By the time the manuscript was finished, I felt that I had lived my previous life all over again. My body ached and my insides were numb. Yet I'm glad I did it—because the book contains a message that every divorced parent with angry, hurting children needs to clip and tuck under the pillow: No matter how bleak the future seems, don't give up hope. Yes, divorce-shattered relationships can be mended—with commitment, determination, patience, and cautious action.

Jay and Grant, my sons, at first were puzzled about the reasons for my being asked to write this book. Why would anybody be interested in us? they asked. But as we examined the emotional roller coaster to which all of us had seemed chained for so long, they understood and they supported my efforts, spending countless hours with me sharing their feelings.

It was difficult for them, too, but I believe that they are as proud of the victory as I am. They have good reason to be.

D.S.

Philadelphia

Chapter 1

The Day It Ended
Also Was the Day It Began

At three o'clock on a Thursday afternoon in early December I left my executive editor's office at *The Charlotte News* and walked past the desk of my secretary, Tina Robertson, who looked up from her typewriter, forced a tight smile, and said, "Good luck."

"Thanks," I said. "It'll be a long afternoon. I wish it were over with."

"Is there anything else I can do?" Tina Robertson was more than a secretary. During the months that had led up to this day, she had listened patiently, questioned me about the finality of my decision, played devil's advocate about the wisdom of my decision. Then, convinced that this was how it was going to be, she had attended to the housekeeping with her unsurpassed efficiency.

"Is the telephone in?" I asked.

"The phone company will be there tomorrow—sometime before noon."

"What about the furniture?"

"The rental company promised to deliver everything by late today. They seemed positive."

"What about the carpet? Did they get that cleaned? Is it going to be dry enough so they can move in the furniture?"

"Yes, it's going to be all right." She banged her hand against the end of the typewriter, bit her lower lip, and said: "Don't worry . . . Can you believe that? I was going to tell you not to worry. Well, good luck . . . and if you need anything else, call me."

"Thanks, Tina. I'll see you in the morning—I hope."

I hustled through the newsroom clutter, out into the lobby, and down four flights of steps on the escalator, my briefcase banging against my right knee. Then I was into the parking garage and beside *my* car, the three-year-old Opel GT that was flame orange on the outside, soft black on the inside, and that contrasted vividly in color, size, and shape with the quiet white Buick station wagon when it was parked in the driveway at home in the suburbs.

My wife of almost twenty-two years, Verna, never liked the pizzazz of the sports car, which in her mind seemed to symbolize the disintegration of the responsible, conservative man she had married and his entrance into the mid-life crisis—and every bit of the craziness that went with it.

"That's a car for a kid," she had said. "*You'll* look silly in it; *I'll* feel silly in it."

But I had bought it anyway, trading in a five-year-old Mustang and promising her that the next year I would exchange her five-year-old Ford wagon for a new one.

"You mean that we have to go through another summer in this old car so you can have the car you want? Don't you ever think of anybody but yourself? What about me and the boys?"

I reminded her that it was the boys, Jay and Grant, in the hotbed of adolescence, who first had brought the Opel GT to my attention, who had pasted pictures of the car on the refrigerator door, who had left notes under the telephone, on my pillow, and on top of the television set proclaiming: "Opel GT, yea; Mustang, boo."

When I told them I didn't think I should buy a car that seated only two persons, they weren't fazed. "It's OK; we'll take turns riding in it," they had said. On weekends the three of us had toured Buick agency showrooms to look at the Opel GT selection, fondling the padded vinyl upholstery and the four-speed gearshift, rotating the concealed headlights into position, remarking that the car truly was what the teenagers called it—"mini-Vette," a shrunk-down version of the famed Chevrolet Corvette. Then we bought the orange one, and our first trip together was to the gasoline station—with all three of us somehow jammed into the cockpit.

It was a happy time, one that we had savored and often talked about: "Hey, do you remember how crowded it was, and Daddy kept yelling that one of us was sitting on the gearshift?" And we had laughed . . . in a rare instance when the three of us seemed totally tuned in together, united, almost as if we were one. Jay's unbending allegiance to his mother had wavered—a little bit, anyway—and when she complained about the absurdity of the tiny orange car, he shrugged it off with "Oh, Mother." When the Cadillac-hoarding woman next door told us that she would "rather have a picture of a car than own an Opel," Jay responded with cheerful, if not completely original, humor: "Sticks and stones may dent our Opel, but words will never harm it."

It was the car in which Jay and Grant learned to use a clutch, Jay haltingly and falteringly, Grant eagerly and quickly. In a way it was symbolic of how they approached new things in life. Jay tended to cling to the familiar; Grant reached out with curiosity and wonder. They were as different as day and night . . . and they always had been.

* * * * *

The symphony of horns at the intersection startled me back to the here and now and told me that I was sitting through a green light. I shifted the car into motion, and the growl of the first gear quickly surrendered to the whine of the fourth gear as I spun onto the expressway and headed south. Within the next two hours I was going to confront the most terrible time of my life and, while I had prepared, I felt strangely unprepared.

I had done my homework. I had talked with many men who had been there, and I had accepted the truth of their unanimous advice: "No matter how bad you think it's going to be, it will be worse. No matter how much you think it will hurt, it will hurt more." I clenched my teeth until my jaws ached and chanted over and over: "It'll be OK; it'll be OK; it'll be . . ."

What causes a marriage to wither and die? In my mind I couldn't point a finger at any one identifiable thing and say, "Yes, that's it; that's what caused our marriage to fail." The words of another man in my situation described my feelings better than I could:

16

"It's a wrenching experience to realize that your love for your wife has dried up, that your heart is cold and your insides empty. It's a position filled with self-hate and self-pity. So drag yourself out, kick yourself, and tell yourself that you just won't have it this way. And you go."

Right now I was going . . . and I was dragging. Ours was a marriage in which we never seemed to achieve a balance—never 50-50 or even 60-40. Rather, it seemed to be mostly 80-20, with the one of us who was on top trying to hold down the other, with the one of us who was on the bottom scratching and gouging to dislodge the other. I had my career, and I would tell her, "This is important to me, and I've got to give it a lot of my time." She had her charismatic religion, and she would tell me, "Until you know God the way I do, you'll never have any peace." No matter who said what to whom, we seemed to argue, two people who forever were kinder to everybody else than to themselves and each other.

Up ahead, I saw Eckerd's drugstore, where Grant worked three afternoons a week after school. And, yes, there was the station wagon in the parking lot, right in front of the store. I parked the Opel next to the wagon and debated if I should go inside and tell Grant that I was leaving the clutch car for a while and taking the wagon. No, if I did that, he'd want to know why—and Eckerd's drugstore wasn't the place for that explanation. I'd just borrow the wagon, and then tomorrow I'd sit down with him and talk about everything.

The Buick felt obscenely huge as I wheeled it out of the lot and onto the back roads that led to the pine-blessed subdivision in which Verna and I eight years earlier had built our dream house—the place where our boys would grow up, a New England saltbox of Canadian cedar that had been stained mustard yellow, a house so breathtakingly handsome that passersby sometimes stopped to gape and those who were more courageous beckoned me away from the zoysia grass that I so often plugged and asked, "Could we come inside and look around?"

It was a house in which we had invested not only our money but also our ideas—and ourselves. The family room opened onto the patio with a Dutch door which, when the top half was unlatched, permitted our cat Allie to jump in and out at his leisure. The family room and kitchen windows were made to fit shutters that had been torn out of an old barn in Indiana and painstakingly painted, antiqued, fly-specked, and varnished by all of us, at one time or another, over the years. The firebox in the fireplace was especially large—because that's how we wanted it—so that we could stoke up a blaze big enough to burn down Chicago.

In the boys' bathroom, between their bedrooms, we had insisted on two washbasins—side by side, one for each of them—so that in the years ahead they would be able to shave at the same time. The contractor had stared at the two little boys with the fuzzy cheeks, and he had shaken his head in amazement that anybody planned a house that meticulously and that far ahead, but he had produced two washbasins, side by side.

Jay and Grant had jumped in disbelief. For years they had moved around—from a modest house we had built in Jefferson City, Missouri, to an aging house we had bought but quickly sold in Louisville, Kentucky, to an apartment, to a marvelous colonial house we had built in Louisville, and finally to an apartment in Charlotte, North Carolina. Now the dream house was a reality and there would be no more moving. I liked my job, and all of us liked Charlotte, a pleasant family town of 250,000 that sprawled like a young, vigorous giant five miles above the South Carolina state line, almost midway between the Great Smoky Mountains to the west and the Atlantic Ocean to the east.

"You mean we'll still be here when I'm big enough to shave?" Jay had asked.

"Long after that," I had answered. "This is home for us."

I had plunged into the role of suburban husband with uncustomary vigor. In the springtime I had walked the damp woodlands behind the house, listening to the wind whistle through the pines and marking with string the flowering dogwoods and redbuds that colored the primitive hillsides. Then in the winter I had returned, sought out the barren trees that bore my pieces of string and dug them up, carefully, lovingly, and transplanted them to the front yard and the side yard. I had fertilized them, mulched them, watered them, and rejoiced in the springtime when the buds blossomed into the fullness of white and pink.

I had bought 250 plugs of zoysia grass from a mail-order nursery in Maryland, and in the early years I had plugged them into the crabgrass of our lawn and waited expectantly for them to take over—as the catalog had promised. Miraculously, it had happened, and then with the part of the yard on the far side of the driveway a carpet of plushy green, I had begun the springtime ritual of transplanting—digging plugs from there and gouging them into the crabgrass on the other side. Grant had been there beside me— every spring, it seemed—as we wielded the heavy iron pluggers that wore blisters on our hands through our leather-faced gloves.

It was hard, draining work, but in the quiet of twilight when I lay in the thick grass with a glass of wine and wrestled with Jay and Grant and Sherman, our red-eyed basset hound, I found sometimes a contentment that was far more intoxicating than the wine.

But that, I thought as the mustard-yellow house came into sight, was so very long ago and far away. Contentment, like so many good things, is fleeting as the wind. Just when you think you have it, you find that it has eluded you, slipped from your grasp as if it never existed. The only residue to remind you that it once was there is in your mind—in the memories that you forever will cherish.

I pulled the wagon into the driveway, alongside the basketball goal with the tattered net, and got out. I started to walk through the garage and into the family room, but the door opened unexpectedly, and there was Verna, looking apprehensive.

"You have the station wagon. Why?"

"I need it to carry some of my things."

"Why?"

"I'm leaving."

* * * * *

A month before, I had decided that at last the time had come to end the marriage to the woman I had dated since I was a college sophomore, a marriage that in the beginning had seemed as good as anybody else's but that had begun to nosedive way back in Louisville, when I was night city editor for *The Courier-Journal* and scratching mightily to climb up the ladder. For a while I had accepted it as the way it was—two people who were developing their own special interests and separate identities and who didn't need the cloying closeness that surely would retard personal growth.

But I was trying to deceive myself, and I knew it. No, we had to bring ourselves back toward each other, and, in the beginning in Charlotte, when we knew nobody and we were totally dependent on each other, we had begun to close the gap. But we never quite made it, not because we were unwilling but because we were unable.

"I wish you wouldn't spend so much time at the office and work so hard," Verna would say. "It's not good for you—or for us. The boys need you."

"It won't be like this forever—the long hours," I would say. "I'll have things in shape in a year or two, and then I can take some time off, and we'll do some things as a family." But I doubted that it was going to happen, and I had the feeling that she knew it wasn't going to happen. Instead of confronting it, we avoided it—as we did most of the trouble spots of our marriage. The inevitable happened: the wounds festered and the contamination spread.

Marriage counseling hadn't helped. In fact, it seemed only to point up the differences that separated us. The arguments were often but they seldom were loud. After all, the boys would hear us, and what would they think? But the boys knew, and one day, in the zoysia grass, Jay had remarked, "I wish you and Mother didn't argue so much."

"I wish so, too, Jay."

"Why don't you stop?"

It was a question for which I had no answer. Was there a reason why intelligent people couldn't live in peace—or at least coexist without the verbal armaments of war? Or was the marriage hopelessly down the drain and was I kidding myself when I wondered if it was as bad as it seemed?

My parents had visited from Missouri in the last November of the marriage, and late one evening, when everybody else was in bed, I had gone to their room to explain to them that time was running out.

"This is the last visit when you'll be able to see all of us in the same house," I said. "It's not working, and it can't ever work. I'm going to leave."

Pop had been jarred. "I've never seen a family torn apart any more than this one, but you've got to think of the boys. Can't you put your troubles behind you—at least until they're older?"

"Oh, you're asking me to mortgage the next five years of my life. I can't do that. I can't and I won't."

"Well, you've got to do what your heart tells you. What's the matter? What's really the matter?"

"I'm miserable. It's been so long since I've loved that I'm not sure I'm still capable of loving. It's like I've lost it through lack of use, like an arm that withers when it's in a cast."

"It's that bad?"

"It's that bad."

"What about the boys?"

"Pop, I have friends who divorced their wives, guys who loved their kids, too. I've asked them how they could leave, and do you know what every one of them said? They all said that when it gets bad enough, you can leave and even your concern for your kids doesn't keep you from leaving. Every one of them told me that the kids are more malleable than we are, that they can absorb the punches and bounce back. I can't absorb any more punches, Pop. The kids are going to have to look out for themselves . . . at least for a while. I'll fix it with them later. I promise I will. But right now I've got to leave. I'm trying to stay alive. If I don't leave, I'll die."

"I can't tell you what to do. But you know how I feel about the boys. They're good kids, and they deserve a father. They *need* a father."

"They'll have a father, Pop. I promise . . ."

He had looked at me sternly but lovingly and nodded, his eyes brimming with tears. Mom had hugged him and hugged me and cried softly. "You know we'll always love you."

"Pop, when you were here last summer, we sat under that big pine tree and you told me that one of your lifelong rules had been never to judge anybody until you had walked in his moccasins. That's what I'm asking. Don't judge me now. Please don't. I'm running for my life, and I can't carry you with me. I've got to do it alone."

"I know . . . I know. Some things we have to do alone. But be careful."

Two days later I put them on the airplane to fly

back to Missouri, and we had hugged and cried, not because we were parting but because our hearts were breaking. Never again would our worlds be the same ... and we mourned that loss—quietly, right in the airport, among the many who milled around, oblivious to our presence.

"Good luck," Pop had said. "We love you."

* * * * *

The morning of the last day of my marriage was like every other day: the alarm went off at six thirty, and I shaved and showered while Jay and Grant dressed and ran for the school bus and Verna cleared the dishes and scrambled an egg for me.

She has to know what's about to happen, I told myself. I ate my egg and toast in silence and then asked that she and the boys be home in midafternoon. I would be coming home then, and I wanted to talk with them. Yes, it was important, and I would appreciate their being at home.

No, there was no doubt: she knew. Her expression told me that she knew—a fearful look that I had seen before, when we had argued and I had stomped out of the house in search of an all-night movie.

Yes, she would be home in midafternoon, and Jay would be home, too, right after school. But it was a workday for Grant. He would be at Eckerd's until evening. Did I want her to call and tell him not to report for work? No, that wouldn't be necessary.

"What do you want to talk about?" she asked.

"I'll tell you this afternoon."

It was a crazy game of cat and mouse that I played because this was a quiet war—and all the rules had to be thrown out the window. If I tipped my hand, I might have to pay the price, and the price could be that I would find myself locked out of my own house, unable to retrieve my clothes, some towels, bed linens, and a few dishes and pieces of silverware. It had happened to one of my friends.

"I'll tell you this afternoon," I repeated as I walked swiftly through the family room into the garage. I opened the garage door for what I knew would be the last time in my life, and I drove away, capturing the mustard-yellow house in the rearview mirror until it disappeared around the curve.

The workday was terrible—plain awful terrible. Tina Robertson, my secretary, walked on eggshells, because she seemed to sense my preoccupation and fright.

"You want me to bring you some coffee?" she asked.

"Yes," I said, but when she returned with it, I didn't drink it. I tried, but it had the taste of ashes. I walked into the managing editor's office for the news conference.

"You look tired," he said.

"I am tired."

"You look terrible."

"I feel terrible."

Halfway through the news conference, during the city editor's report, I left and wandered back into my office, closed the door, pulled shut the draperies on the glass wall to seal out the newsroom, and stared at the montage of pictures behind my desk. There was a print of the orange-colored tiger made with a linoleum block by Jay in the seventh grade. There was a photograph of Grant, taken from behind the catcher, as he unwound in a Little League game and hurled a baseball toward the plate. They were all there—memories of an adult lifetime—and I turned away, flopped down on my couch, and focused on the ceiling, trying not to think about anything.

The minutes dragged by as if time itself had been unplugged. Finally, three o'clock arrived, and I trudged out of my office, not totally sure if I felt like the executioner or the victim. Tina told me good-bye, and I left, wishing her a nice day in a voice that seemed to croak from dryness. The time had come.

* * * * *

Verna knew, but she didn't want to know. "You have the station wagon. Why?"

"I need it to carry some of my things."

"Why?"

"I'm leaving."

"Oh, no . . . you can't . . . You can't leave. It's not that bad. It's not."

"I'm not doing this on the spur of the moment. I've thought about it. It's best for all of us. It really is . . ."

She was crying, but her voice was controlled. "Look, if you want more time to yourself, if you want privacy, we can fix the front bedroom for you. We won't bother you at all and—"

"No, that's not it. Look, this is something I have to do—for myself."

"What have I done?" Her voice was starting to break.

"It's what *we* have done . . . to each other . . . for so many years. Look, I've got to pack some things. There's really nothing for us to talk about. It's all

26

been said. I'm sorry." My voice was soft—the way it becomes when I'm emotional or frightened. Now I was both emotional and frightened, and it was becoming difficult for me to say anything.

I brushed past her and slammed into the family room, where Jay stood, a tall, slender young man in jeans and a blue V-neck sweater. I saw him, and I started crying.

"Jay, I'm sorry that it's come to this. Jay, I'm moving away, but it's not your fault. It's your mother and I. We haven't . . . Well, you must know we've been having problems."

Jay seemed to have a mask on his face, which revealed no emotion at all—no pain, no anguish, not even surprise.

"I don't know why you have to leave," he said slowly. "I'd think that two grown people could work out their differences."

"Jay, I've got to do this. I don't expect you to understand now, but you will—eventually. I promise you will. Oh, Jay, dammit, I love you and Grant so much . . . and it's killing me . . . killing me to leave the two of you. I don't want to leave you, but I have to . . ."

The mask remained in place. "If you love us, I don't see why you're leaving. People don't leave people they love. It doesn't make any sense."

The tears washed down my face, and I found myself unable to talk anymore. I had miscalculated badly. In my inexperience I had believed that I would be capable of rational conversation, that I could answer Jay's questions so that he at least could accept the reality of what was happening if not grasp the reasons why. But I was failing, drowning in a whirlpool of emotionality.

"Jay, I'll talk to you later, and I'll explain. Please, don't judge me now. Try not to judge me. I love you . . . and this is killing me."

"It's killing me, too," Jay said, still as expressionless as before. "This is something I'll never forget—not for the rest of my life. It's killing me, too."

I vaulted the steps to the master bedroom and began throwing clothes onto the bed from the closet. Verna was beside me, crying, too, and pleading for me to read the note that she was trying to stick into my hand.

"I can't read anything," I sobbed.

"Please read it. Please. I can write it . . . but I can't say it."

I sat on the bed, amid the scattering of trousers and jackets, and tried to read the note, which said that she loved me and that she'd rather die than have the family break up.

"Oh, God, stop it!" I screamed. "Stop it! We're at a dead end. The family broke up years ago. We've lived together, but we haven't been a family for so long. Surely you recognize that. I've got to leave. I *am* leaving."

I stumbled down the stairs and to the car with an armload of clothing. Then another . . . and another. Then the golf bag and portable television.

"You really are leaving, aren't you?" Verna asked. "You've really made up your mind, and there's nothing we can do, is there?" The tears had gone, and now the anger seemed to be building. "Well, then go ahead and leave—if that's what you want."

"It's what I want because there's nothing else to do. I'm sorry. I'm sorry it's come to this. I'm sorry we've run out of options. I'll see that you have enough money. I'll send you a check every month, but I want you to see a lawyer. For your own protection, I want you to see a lawyer."

"Why? You'll be back in a while, won't you?"

I had been wrong again. She didn't really understand. She thought I was leaving in anger—like for an all-night movie—and that it was not forever.

"I want you to see a lawyer," I repeated. "It's something you need to do."

"I don't need a lawyer. I trust you. I know you'll be fair."

The sky had turned December black by the time I left, and again, as I had that very morning, I watched the outline of the house in the rearview mirror fade around the corner as I guided the station wagon out to the main road.

It was over with—at least the first awful amputation. Tomorrow I would see Grant at work . . . and he would understand. Of all the people in the world he would understand.

I unloaded the station wagon at my tiny $175-a-month apartment and then drove back to Eckerd's to pick up the Opel. My next stop was to deliver a dinner speech to a church couples club that was holding its Christmas meeting at a Holiday Inn off Interstate 85. Oh, how long ago I had agreed to speak on this evening. Oh, how I wished that it could have been any other time. But here I was, driving toward the interstate and mulling over the theme of the talk that I had drafted: The road to happiness is paved with honesty to ourselves and others. I thought I would choke. I didn't see how I could stand up and talk, but I did. And when I finished, they applauded and told me how sorry they were that my wife couldn't be there to hear me.

* * * * *

It was three thirty in the afternoon of the next day when I walked into Eckerd's in search of Grant . . . and there he was, punching keys in a cash register and explaining to a customer that the price marked on the roll of paper towels was wrong and that it really cost a dime more. I waited, off to the side, until the customer left, and then I approached Grant, my heart pounding with uncertainty.

"Grant, can we talk for a minute?"

He looked right through me as if to ask: What do we have to talk about? But he said nothing.

"Grant, please, I need to talk to you."

"I'm busy. Can't you see I'm busy?" Then he turned and called to another boy: "Bobby, can you run this register for a minute? I've got to do some things in the back of the store." And he walked away. I pursued him.

"Grant, I'm sorry. Just listen to me—"

"I don't want to talk to you."

"Grant, if you'll just listen . . . please . . ."

"You left us. You left *me*. How could you do that? Why?"

He walked back to the cash register, at which a line of customers had formed, and he told Bobby that he was ready to take over again.

He began ringing up the purchases, banging the

30

keys, and sacking the goods, determined not to look at me.

"Grant . . ."

He *wouldn't* look at me. There would be no more talking today. I staggered from the store, blinded by tears, and finally I reached the security of the Opel GT. I drove away, but in two blocks I had to pull off and park. I was hysterical, and the tears were so thick I couldn't see the road anymore.

I looked into the rearview mirror and studied the flushed face that stared back at me, a face twisted in agony and grief, and I wondered why not even my closest friends had told me that the pain would seem life-threatening. To break up a family somebody had to be either very crazy or very courageous—and at that instant I wasn't certain into which group I fit. I couldn't imagine how I ever could drive the car back to the apartment, but I did . . . finally.

Chapter 2

A Kind of Love Letter

Dear Verna:

In the many years of our marriage one of my favorite expressions was "What's happening?" After work I'd walk into our house, during the early years, and you'd be in the kitchen and I'd holler, "What's happening?" Your answer always was as predictable as my question: "Supper's happening. Are you hungry?" Now as the wreckage settles in the muck around us, I'm wondering not what is happening but what has happened. What happened to us? What happened to a love that surely was as strong as most and stronger than many?

When I was in the Army, before we were married, you'd ride with Pop to Fort Leonard Wood to visit me on weekends during my basic training. I so looked forward to your coming . . . and later in my desperation to be with you I sometimes considered, when the sergeant pulled my pass, trying to ride off the post in the trunk of a friend's car. I never did, of course, but I thought about it . . . because I thought about you.

After the Army, in the first year of our marriage, we settled into our first apartment. It was only two rooms and a tiny kitchen on the second floor, but to us it was the grandest apartment there ever was. We curled up on the little old couch and watched *Playhouse 90* on our boxlike television with its black-and-white picture that seemed so large then. We wanted nothing more than we had—because we had each other.

When friends visited, sometimes friends of mine from the Army, you always cooked spaghetti and meat sauce, and for dessert you made orange sherbet—because that's the only dinner you knew how to fix then. Later you became a grand hostess and a splendid cook, but nothing ever tasted better to me than spaghetti, meat sauce, and orange sherbet. My friends envied me, and they told me so, because you and I seemed so happy together. It was the kind of marriage they wanted, they said, and if they were lucky, someday they might have it.

Do you remember the nights we slept on the daybed on the screened-in porch, off the kitchen? Sometimes, especially in the spring, it rained hard, and the water seeped through the old roof and pattered down on us. We'd snatch up the bed linens and flee inside, hand in hand, giggling, like two little kids who loved each other very much.

We were in our first house, you remember, when you became pregnant with Jay, and we'd lie together in bed and feel him kick against your stomach wall and imagine that he was crying, "Let me out of here right now!" Who could have been happier—or more excited—than we were during those moments? Nobody. Absolutely nobody.

Jay was born, and his first snowsuit was pale green, and we were so proud when we took him out to visit.

On his first haircut, you cried, and I scooped some of his hair off the barbershop floor and saved it. I still have it—along with the newspaper story I wrote.

The favorite game we played with Jay . . . and then with Grant . . . was, well, you remember, don't you? We called it "mousy-creep," and we'd run our fingers up their ribs as they lay face up on the bed and giggled in anticipation, even before our fingers arrived.

You remember the wooden rocking horse, too, don't you? Its name was Tee-Gum, because that was what Jay called it—and Grant, too, when he was old enough to know what it was. The nights we walked the floor together when they were sick—one or both of them—were terrifying nights, because in our youth we imagined that every sickness was much worse than it really was. But the terror brought us closer together. We were a family.

Where did we begin to lose what we once had? What happened to two young people in love who gradually—yet so suddenly—became middle-aged strangers? Sometimes I wonder why we ever got married. I can't tell you why—except that I felt I needed you and that without you I might never have another chance at the happiness I thought our relationship could bring. As the years went by and as we drifted farther apart, I asked myself if perhaps you, too, felt that marrying me might be your only chance for happiness. But by then we had stopped talking to each other about much of anything, and I never asked you. Maybe you felt as bad about yourself as I felt about myself. Maybe we both drowned trying to save ourselves.

I'm sorry for the times I hurt you. I could see the hurt burned into your eyes as we faced each other that Sunday night at the close of our Marriage Encounter weekend and repeated our marriage vows. You cried, but I didn't. Perhaps by then I had already run out of tears . . . and feelings.

I know you're sorry, too—sorry for your participation, willing and unwilling, in our awful ritual of disengagement over the years. But now, being sorry doesn't help—for me or for you. It's too late—too late even to be sorry.

I wish you happiness. I wish myself happiness, too. But most of all, I wish happiness for our sons. I hope that they forever can avoid the tragedy that we could not and that they can embrace the longtime comfort of togetherness that somehow slipped away from us. They always will be part of us—even though we no longer are part of each other.

I hope we can be friends someday.

Darrell

Chapter 3

The Way We're Bent
Is the Way We Grow

It is preached by some that what happens to us is predestined—not necessarily in the sense that a divine being orchestrates the details of our lives but in the sense that an acorn must grow into an oak tree. For years I feared that I was an acorn, and doggedly I struggled to escape becoming the oak tree that was my father.

He deserved more out of life than he received. He knew it and he was bitter about it for many years—a kind of bitterness that seemed to contaminate his inherent decency and sweetness. I wanted more from life, and I knew that to achieve more I had to be willing to take some risks, to step from light into darkness and grope with uncertainty until I found my way.

"Why can't you be satisfied with what you have—rather than always wanting more?" he asked. When I tried to explain it to him, he seemed not to understand. My response was to back away, and his response to that was to feel pain from what he perceived as my lack of concern and love.

For years we were not close—emotionally as well as geographically. But then we both changed—independent changes that reshaped and revitalized our relationship.

His change came in the last two decades of his life, when he made peace with himself and when the Great Depression finally was more an awful memory than a blatant robber that stalked his every step. When he discovered himself, he discovered me, too—in the sense that he understood, enough at least so that he comfortably could accept.

My change came in the crush of mid-life, when I seemed to have everything but when I felt that I had nothing. In the unraveling of that, I stopped the struggle against myself and against him too. Then I recognized the beauty and strength of the old oak tree.

* * * * *

The man was almost eighty years old, but he was still tall and erect, and in the thirteen years since his retirement he had stayed active and, with the luxury of unlimited time, had done the things that he had waited much of his life to do.

He read books and magazines with an intellectual hunger that was a joy for his wife to watch; he planted and harvested his little garden behind the modest brick house on which the mortgage long ago had been settled; he studied the Bible. And every day, as he had since the very beginning, he told his wife of almost fifty-four years that he loved her.

On this day he had spaded ground for the tomatoes that he was going to plant. He had eaten heartily at the supper table, and then he and his wife had attended a meeting of the Full Gospel Business Men's Fellowship. Now they walked from the meeting half a block to their maroon car with the cream-colored top, a 1966 Ford sedan that was as spotless as the basement in which it was garaged.

Suddenly the man stopped, gasped, and clutched a parking meter for support. "I—I don't think I can walk anymore. I don't feel well." Somebody who had followed him out of the meeting guided him to the car. "I need help," he calmly told his wife. "I need oxygen . . . I can't breathe."

He slumped forward, then straightened up and seemed to acknowledge the ambulance siren that knifed through the cool Missouri evening. His wife, wide-eyed with fear, tried to be calm. She rubbed his back and told him, "Hang in there, Pop; help is coming." Then the ambulance took him away.

At the hospital a doctor told the wife that they were doing all they could but that the man wasn't responding. Then, ten minutes later, the doctor reappeared, dropped to his knees, clutched the woman's icy hands, and said: "I'm so sorry; he's gone. We just couldn't do enough. We tried . . . Oh, God, how we tried, but . . ."

The woman sat quietly, too stunned to cry, her heart racing and her chest aching. Even in the room where a dozen other people waited, she felt so terribly alone. They asked if she wanted them to do anything, and she said, "Would you please call our son in Philadelphia?"

* * * * *

My telephone rang at five minutes past midnight, and they told me that Pop was dead. Then they put Mom on the line and she said, very softly and very calmly: "Please come home. I need you."

It was a telephone call that, intellectually, I knew would come sometime. Pop had told me the year before that time was running out for him, that he had lived almost a decade beyond his allotted threescore and ten years. But emotionally I wasn't ready for it. Red-eyed and hoarse, I whispered, "I thought he'd live forever."

* * * * *

Pop bore his legacy from the Great Depression the way a boxer wears the evidence of his confrontations—all over his mind and body. He discussed it; he understood it; he forever was affected by it. For much of his life the trauma seemed all-pervasive. He was a college man—unlike most in his day—but that didn't protect him when the Wabash Railroad, for which he worked, began to tighten its belt and consolidate jobs. He was laid off when I was five months old, and for the next two years he worked a total of four months. He lost the house in which I was born, and he was forced to sell every stick of furniture that he and Mom owned. He talked about it with me on more than one occasion, when I asked, and his perspective added to the Depression a dimension that I never found in any history book.

"I had $400 in $20 bills and that's all the money we had in the world. I carried it with me because the banks were busted and there was no place to deposit it. That's the worst time we ever had—not the relationship between Mom and me but the daily worry of what would happen when the money was gone and I still had no job. Each time I'd break a $20 bill, I'd count what I had left and mentally figure how much longer we could go and still keep food on the table. I look back now and realize that during that time Mom could have taken you and gone back to her parents on the farm in Arkansas. They had plenty of food and plenty of room, but she never even discussed it and I don't think she ever thought about it."

Pop tried to get work—how hard he tried—but most of the time he couldn't even get an interview. Many of the companies had guards at their doors and when they found that somebody was looking for work, they made it plain that he was not welcome. It was heartbreaking . . . and terrifying.

By cutting corners we got by on less than $4 a week for food, Pop said, after dropping all our life insurance—except for two 25-cent-a-week policies that he had taken out in my name. The daily diet we ate was austere—mostly soup and apples—but it was nourishing, and affordable. We could make a kettle of good soup for about a quarter, and Mom seemed to bake apples day and night, because apples could be bought for a dollar a bushel.

The grocery stores, Pop said, ran weekly specials on rabbits, which hung by the dozens, with their insides removed, their heads down, and their hides undisturbed. Rabbits sold for 15 cents each, and before long we were buying them and eating them. Turnips were 40 cents a bushel, and sometimes we bought them by the bushel. If anybody had as much as $5 to spend on groceries—and almost nobody did—it wasn't possible to spend it at a store and carry home everything in one load. But that was little consolation to the many who didn't have $5.

For a while after the house was repossessed, we lived in two rented rooms for $8 a month in a smoky little town in north-central Missouri. But then Pop no longer could afford $8, and we moved into one room for $4 a month. Pop never seemed to want to talk about that but, if I pressed him, he would go into detail.

Our one room had in it a daybed that had to be propped up on one side to keep us from slipping off, a wooden box that was the stand on which we kept our oil lamp, a rickety table, and a two-burner oilstove. For a while Pop tried to raise some chickens, and he fixed up a little place for them and bought some feed. But after he sold them he realized that he had spent more for feed than he had earned from the chickens—and he never tried it again.

We survived, perhaps better than most families, Pop said, because we didn't have as much to lose as many others. "It taught me that a man can get along if he makes up his mind. I guess that's what in later years always made me sort of a miser. At least I always thought you felt that I was awfully tight with the money when you were growing up. That's why. I got that way back then when I learned not to spend a penny I didn't have to spend."

The most heartbreaking part of the story was still to come, and Pop shared it with me only once—not because he was unwilling but because I didn't want to hear it again. When he finished the story, I was sobbing, and I excused myself, stood on the front porch, and wondered how on earth a man could survive that kind of adversity.

Pop had landed a part-time job as a clerk in a grocery store, and the $8 a week he averaged not only put food on the table but also brought joy to his heart. He was working again.

"One of my jobs every night was to soak the stale wieners in vinegar. That made them look plump and fresh the next day when we put them back in the meat counter. I don't know how they tasted, but nobody ever brought one back and complained. I didn't like to do it, and it really bothered me because it wasn't honest. Finally, I mustered my courage and told the boss that I couldn't do it anymore. He looked at me and said without blinking, 'Then we'll hire somebody who can do it.' That night he fired me, and it was Christmas Eve, 1933. I went home to Mom, and it was the blackest night of my life. I thought I'd die—and for a while I didn't even care. Yes, I did care, but what was happening really was terrible. I just couldn't see the end of it. People all around us were scared and getting hungry, and no relief was available except local welfare and there wasn't much they could do with such a big problem."

During that bleak, dreary winter the Government started some relief work, the first part of which was known as the CWA—for Civil Works Administration. Pop applied for a bookkeeper's job after he heard that an opening existed, but he quickly was told that no job existed. He was at the bottom of the barrel, and he went to the welfare office and asked for help. His description of that event forever stayed with me.

"I walked in and there were people I knew— people just like me—standing there at the window asking for handouts. There were people you wouldn't expect to see there—people who'd had $400-a-month jobs in the good days. We all stood there like sheep-killing dogs, too embarrassed to look at each other, and stared at the floor. I got a book of script for $2.50 worth of groceries, and I told them that if they could help me get a job over at the CWA office, I wouldn't ever be back to see them. I don't know if that made any difference, but the next day I got a call and went to work for $15 a week. I did the office work for the CWA workers, who were out in the parks or anyplace that looked as though some improvements could be made. The workers made a maximum of $10.80 a week, and they included ex-railroad firemen and people from all other occupations—all out there doing what had to be done to get that $10.80."

But that job played out, too, and when it did, Pop felt that he was at the end of his rope. His body's response was not to accept food. Because of the resulting weight loss and jitters Pop checked into a tiny hospital, where a physician with a tiny heart told him: "Your nerves are shot. You're a wreck. You'll never be able to do a full day's work again."

Pop, they decided, had suffered from a nervous breakdown. He couldn't handle the storm, and his system had cracked. In those days it was more socially acceptable to jump out a window than to suffer a nervous breakdown when things got too bad. If a man lost a fortune on the stock market and leaped to his death, people talked about it: "It's a shame what happened to Bill, isn't it?" But if a man broke apart at the emotional seams, people didn't talk. They whispered: "Poor Charlie, it was too much for him. They say he'll never be the same."

But Charlie Sifford fooled them. He was down, all

right, but he wasn't out. He found a job and moved us from Moberly to Jefferson City, Missouri, the state capital, where I would grow up. He had no money in the bank, but he had steady work—and that's all he needed. His stomach no longer flipped and flopped. He ate well and he slept well. He felt like Charlie Sifford used to feel back in the good old days. But the good times didn't last long. His boss, like that physician, also had a tiny heart, and he used the scar tissue of the Great Depression the way some men used whips.

As the work load increased, he didn't add more people. He simply piled more work on Pop, and, as the overload took its toll, as Pop fell farther and farther behind, he told Pop, "If you can't handle things, I'll get somebody else." The fear of losing yet another job filled Pop with a terror that drove him to work ten or twelve or fourteen hours a day, six and sometimes seven days a week. Often he'd come home for dinner and then return to the office in the evening, and I'd go with him. I'd take a book, and he would get out his pencil and adding machine and tackle the mounds of paper before him. Sometimes, when I'd look up from a book, I'd see Pop with his head down and sometimes he would mumble what sounded like, "It's too much . . . too much."

His stomach began to toss and turn again; his weight dropped; his dreams became nightmares. It was as if he could hear the voices out of his past: "Poor Charlie . . . nervous breakdown . . . a wreck . . ."

He took a leave of absence and checked into a St. Louis hospital, and there it was his good fortune to meet a physician with a big, warm heart. Pop wasn't in such bad shape, he told him. All of us have our overload point; it's nature's way of telling us when it's time to back off and slow down. People only can do so much—and to expect them to do more is unrealistic of those who expect it, not of those who are unable to do it.

No, Charlie Sifford wasn't a wreck. He was just a normal guy who was having a normal reaction to abnormally hard times. He needed some rest and some understanding. If his boss couldn't accept that, then Pop needed a new boss. Not everybody out there had a cold and tiny heart. There would be other jobs. He needed to remember that nothing was worth everything. He would be all right. The doctor was confident of that because, after all, Charles Sifford was a survivor. The worst already was behind.

The doctor had been correct. There would be other jobs—within the same organization—with more reasonable bosses. Pop had not cracked; he simply had reacted as any healthy person would react. He had reached his limits, and his body had told him to back away. That wasn't something to be whispered about. That was something to shout from the rooftops. It was what had saved him—and us, his family.

* * * * *

A Philadelphia psychologist who became a personal friend once asked me about my relationship with Mom and Pop, and I answered by reciting the story of what happened when I had an offer to leave my job as managing editor of the Jefferson City *News-Tribune*, at age thirty, and join *The Courier-Journal* in Louisville to work on the copy desk. The move meant leaving home and going four hundred miles away. Yes, I was unhappy in my job and knew that for professional growth and personal happiness I needed to leave, but the first move always is the toughest. Ambivalence was a millstone around my neck. Where could I go for guidance? Yes, that's right—to Pop.

I asked him to come to the back porch, away from everybody else, and I put the question to him like this, "You don't think I should go, do you?"

Yes, Pop responded, he did think that I should go, that the opportunity was too great to pass up. Years later he would tell me the soul-searing agony behind that message.

"It was the hardest thing I ever had to say. It was like I was dying inside, knowing I was helping you decide to move away. But it would have been selfish of me to suggest that you stay so we could see you.

"A parent has to realize, and it's painful, that his life is gone to a large extent but that his children's lives are just beginning. To tie them to parents out of selfishness would be unpardonable. But even so, the temptation to do it is very great. We—your mother and I—had to fight it."

I told that story—and some other stories—to the psychologist, who grasped my arm and told me, "You're lucky to have the parents you have."

* * * * *

Yes, I was lucky in so many ways but less lucky perhaps in one way. Pop's craving was for security—at virtually any price. That's what mattered most to him and, given what happened to him in the Great Depression, I could understand it. But I didn't like it. At some point I must have vowed grimly in my subconsciousness that security would not be my ultimate goal in life. The goal would be to succeed, although at the time I'm not sure what my definition of success would have been. Perhaps it would have resolved around an office with stuffed furniture, color-coordinated draperies, and a stereophonic music system, an executive secretary, a private washroom, and access to the executive dining room. That would be tangible evidence of success—and who could dispute it? I would have to take some risks, but it would be worth it. Anything would be worth it. Pop, because he was so beaten down by circumstance, hadn't received a big bite out of life. I would get a big bite. Nobody would ever do to me what so many seemed to have done to Pop. No, I'd never be on the bottom. I would be a s-u-c-c-e-s-s. I would grow into my own oak tree—not Pop's. I would break the pattern.

Pop never understood the frenzy with which I worked and pursued the holy grail of success for so many years. Once at dinner he asked, "How many people do you suppose become that successful—one in a thousand?" My answer was: "That's OK. I'll be that one."

In one of our sitting-on-the-floor conversations in his final years I told Pop that I was certain that much of my runaway ambition had been the result of my not wanting to be trapped by circumstances and bosses—the way he had been trapped.

It was the one time—in everything we shared—that I wished I had kept my thoughts to myself. Pop's reaction was uncustomarily sharp.

"You seem to be saying that I failed in life," he

said. "I don't see it as a failure."

"I wanted it better than you had it . . . and I knew I'd have to be more aggressive and less conscious of security," I said.

"I did the best I could."

"I know you did, Pop, and I admire you for that, but—"

"It was hard . . . for a lot of years. The Depression took something away from me, but I wasn't a failure. A man can't have a wife like your mother and ever think he didn't succeed."

I put my arms around his neck and kissed him.

* * * * *

The Methodist minister who preached Pop's funeral said that Charles D. Sifford was a "Christian gentleman who lived his religion every day" in his relationships with the people whose lives he touched, in the gentleness and consideration he showed in everything he did.

The minister looked directly at Mom and said, "Surely, Hazel, you know how much he loved you." Then he looked straight at me and said, "Surely, Darrell, you know how proud he was of you."

When the time finally came, I wondered how I would say good-bye to Pop. But as I stood beside the casket for the last time and gazed at Pop's peaceful face, I found that the words just tumbled out: "Well, Pop, we've said it all to each other. Aren't we lucky?" After that I must have cried for three hours, and later, as I sat in the backyard, near the tomato garden, I heaved convulsively and repeated: "I don't know what's wrong with me. I don't know . . ."

A friend grasped my arm and said, "Your father has

died, and you loved him."

Yes, I did love him and, best of all, I had told him so. He knew it, and he had reveled in it—perhaps as only a father can when he hears it from a son. If there is victory for the living, for those who mourn, this is where it comes from—from sharing openly feelings with people who matter very much.

It had taken Pop and me so many years to be open with each other, emotionally, without concern that the other might not understand or might not accept. But when it happened, after we came to terms with ourselves in our own lives, it was as if the floodgates had been thrown open to allow the waters of admiration, respect, and love to wash every crevice of our relationship.

It was an important lesson for me to learn, that openness and lack of defensiveness were what made love possible. I wish I had learned the lesson earlier.

Chapter 4

Marriage: The Grass Roots Can Run Very Deep

Why do we marry the people we marry?

As a newspaper reporter, I sometimes covered the courthouse in my early years, and I was struck by how many times in divorce cases I heard husbands and wives echo what amounted to this: "The marriage was doomed from the start. We just weren't right for each other."

It always made me wonder why those of us who weren't right for each other decided to get married. Why didn't we wait and look for somebody else—somebody who was "right"?

Some of us don't wait, I'm convinced, because we don't recognize that we're about to commit a mistake that will torture us and those we love for what seems to be much of our lifetimes. It's our own fault, psychologist Edward B. Fish once told me, because we don't pay as much attention to picking a mate as we do to buying a car or hiring an employee.

Most of us could do as well, Fish said, if we blindfolded ourselves, stood on a street corner, and tapped for marriage the fifteenth or the fiftieth person who strolled past. If we're fortunate, we marry the right person for the right reasons at the right time, but the probability of this is like winning the super jackpot at Atlantic City.

In other words, we don't have to go to the casinos to gamble for high stakes. We often do it when we select a mate, but for a mile-long list of reasons we many times don't recognize it as a gamble.

The typical woman, it's been said, thinks more about her wedding gown than the man she's marrying. The typical man thinks more about the qualities of a young woman who is applying to be his secretary. He checks out her references before he makes a decision; he doesn't hire her because he falls head over heels for her.

Many of us, the divorce lawyers and marriage counselors lament, throw common sense and sound judgment out the window in matters that relate to love. Why? Because we feel that we lose the element of love if we're too clear about how we choose our love objects.

There are, the experts say, a series of romantic myths that sometimes get us into king-size trouble. Among the myths:

—The idea that a one-and-only person exists for us and that when we think we've found that person, we must grab the person—even in the face of the red flags that fly at full staff.

—The idea that we "fall in love." That's pretty much bunk, everybody seems to agree. We fall into bed, but we don't really fall in love. True love has to grow.

—The notion that love is blind and that love conquers all. This sets us up for a date in divorce court because we tend to think that marriage will mend what we view as the negative parts of ourselves and our spouse. Sometimes love even makes it impossible for us to identify these negatives in the other person—until after the glow wears off.

—The belief that love is a challenge and that if it comes too easily, it can't be real love. This often is a reason why people are attracted to people who are hard to get.

—The long-standing belief that sex and love are so intertwined that if we sleep with somebody, we're duty bound to marry that person. This sounds about as crazy as thinking that you're a failure because you resigned from the football team, but it's really true, the therapists claim.

Basically, the experts seem to agree, we marry people who appear to fulfill our current needs. This is why people who are fearful of being dominated might marry somebody they could dominate and why people who subconsciously need to suffer might marry somebody who will make them suffer. It's also why people who feel that they have failed both themselves and the world might marry somebody who doesn't think that they are failures.

Some other off-the-wall reasons that therapists advance for marriage:

—Proximity. We tend to marry people with whom we have a lot of contact. This is why college is like a mating ground.

—Physical similarities. Strangely, perhaps, we tend to marry somebody who is not too dissimilar from us in appearance.

—Status symbol. It's possible to marry somebody because she looks good and you'll look good when you walk down the street with her. Silly? You bet, but isn't it the kind of silliness with which many of us can identify—if we're honest?

—The time is right. There comes a time, for most of us, when we think that we're ready for marriage, and we're more receptive to marriage. The person we marry might be the same person we hardly noticed a year or two earlier—when the time wasn't right. But at this moment, this is where our needs are, for better or for worse.

* * * * *

The year was 1949, and the war survivors had come back to college, wearing their khaki trousers, fatigue shirts, and white buck shoes with red rubber soles. I wasn't one of them—but I was there with them.

Classes hadn't started yet—in fact, I hadn't even completed registration—but that had no effect on the tempo of football practice. I was among the fifty who clung together, symbolically, in our clean white practice jerseys and waited for somebody to tell us what to do.

We didn't have to wait long. "All right!" a gravelly voice cried. "You freshmen, get over here! We want you to work a little bit against these other people."

The "other people" grinned at us, some of them anyway. They rubbed the palms of their hands together in mock anticipation of what was to follow. However, others seemed to be inspecting their shoelaces, trying desperately to convince themselves that the inevitable really wasn't going to happen. These "other people" were men, combat veterans of World War II, people who had flown forty missions over

Germany, stormed ashore at Normandy, fought and killed in the steaming jungles of the South Pacific. Their average age, I guessed, was the middle to late twenties, but a few of them were in their thirties, brawny, round-chested men whose arms bore tattoos and whose faces carried the invisible scars of war.

As the military liked to say, these were men whose tickets had been punched, men who had been there and back, who had seen it all and who would tell you about it—even if you didn't ask. Mostly they were loud, and frequently they were profane, in a kind of way that I'd never heard before. The college rules were for the rosy-cheeked kids, like me, fresh out of high school—not for the men who had fought the war to end all wars and saved the country. No, they would live and play by their own rules . . . and if the college didn't approve of their smuggling a lot of beer and a few women into the dormitories, then the college was going to have to rethink its position. After all, they were men.

There had been a ruckus just the other day in my dormitory over beer and women. A dormitory counselor who was a graduate student in his early twenties had confronted one of the football players and told him: "You can't do that around here. I'm going to report you, and then you'll be in big trouble." The football player slowly had removed a bridge that held three front teeth, and then he had smiled at the counselor, licking his tongue between the gaps in his teeth. "Let's see now . . . Do I understand this? You're going to make big trouble for me? Is that right? Listen, boy, I spent two years in a prisoner-of-war camp, and I know what big trouble is. Now, you just forget about this and go back and study your little books. Otherwise, you'll be in big trouble—not me. You understand me, boy?"

The counselor had retreated, his tail between his legs, and some of the other football players had jeered, waved, and chanted, "Bye-bye, sweetheart." It was a man's world, and I was smack in the middle of it—as an eighteen-year-old boy with high hopes and the best football scholarship that the University of Missouri offered. Not only did the scholarship pay the rent and buy the meals but it also carried with it a groundskeeping job that kept me in pocket money. And there was another benefit, too, for the special few who had arrived with some fanfare and a lot of promise—as I had. I found out about this benefit the first day that I had showered after practice. As I left the shower, a towel draped around my neck, a man in a brown suit had called my name and thumbed through a stack of white envelopes that he held in his right hand. "Yes . . . here's one for you, son. Good luck." I had opened it, and there was a check for $75—just a little something to tide me over the rough spots between paydays, the man had said after winking slyly.

In the years right after the war this kind of payment wasn't uncommon, and unquestionably it had given rise to the story about the college coach who, at halftime with his team three touchdowns behind, had screamed: "What's the matter with you guys? You're playing like a bunch of amateurs!" The story was old now, and nobody laughed anymore, because it wasn't a joke. It was fact. They paid you to play, and if you didn't play well enough, they cut off the money.

Later on, that would happen to me. I would be coming out of the shower, and there would be the man in the brown suit with the envelopes. But before he could give me the money, an assistant coach would intercept the envelope with my name on it and say blandly, "I believe there's been a mistake here." After that I never again saw the man in the brown suit—or any more $75 checks.

But on this late summer afternoon, I wasn't thinking about money or even about college. I was thinking about survival—and about how college football was so different from what I had expected in so many ways. Here on this sprawling mid-America campus, football was big business. It was what brought in the revenue to finance the other sports—even before the dollar bonanza of television. As freshmen, we had been told very early why our way was being paid through school. A field-house memo had summoned us to a meeting and, to my surprise, the varsity coaches were there, too—in addition to the freshman coaches and their graduate school assistants. The head coach had smiled like a doting father and had said: "Well, men, we all know why you're here: to play football . . . and, of course, to get an education." Somebody near the back of the room had snickered, but the coach's icy stare had cut it off. "As I was saying, you're here to get an education . . . and we, the staff, want to do whatever we can to help you. If you have trouble with your studies, let us know, and we'll arrange special tutoring. If you run short of money, let us know about that, too, and we'll do what we can to help . . . especially with the meals."

The coach swiveled his head and took all of us in

with a single glance. His voice was soft and matter-of-fact: "If you get a girl in trouble, don't be embarrassed to come to us. We've handled things like that before—" A hint of laughter arose, and this time, instead of the icy stare, the coach broke into a grin. It was as if he had granted the freshmen permission to laugh aloud, and some of us did.

"Any questions?" the coach asked. "Anything we can do for you now?"

Silence echoed off the walls.

"Good. Good. Then we'll see you on the practice field."

The meeting had been brief, but it had set the tone for everything that had followed—grim, serious business, and not much fun. In high school, football had been fun, and maybe that's why I had enjoyed playing so much and why I had done so well. We had a coach who believed that to win you had to score more points than the other team, not hold the other team to fewer points than you scored. The emphasis had been on the offense, and we had passed the football . . . and passed . . . and passed. As an end who was quick and sure-handed, I had been the primary receiver, breaking the school records not only for catching passes but also for scoring touchdowns. And that's why the University of Missouri wanted me.

Scholarship offers had been extended from half a dozen schools, but I always had my mind and heart set on the university. It was, after all, the home-state college, and it had the journalism school that I wanted to attend. The head coach, when he heard about the other offers, had sent me a letter that said:

"You're too good to go to any place except the University of Missouri. We're looking forward to having you with us."

My high school coach, who had played at Missouri, had pushed me in that direction and had told me that I was going to make him very proud. Friends had said the same thing. Business people had gone out of their way to assure me that my football success at Missouri was guaranteed and that, after football, I'd have clear sailing in a newspaper career. Everybody would know who I was, they said—the guy who caught all those passes for all those years. So I had signed the letter and accepted the scholarship . . . and now here I was, thinking about survival.

"All right! You freshmen, get over here!" They had split us up into four teams, calling off names from a list on the clipboard, and I was in the first group, a defensive team that was going to challenge the varsity offense. I crouched at left end as the gold-shirted varsity players broke from their huddle and lined up with a flanker just off my left shoulder. I stared at the two-day stubble on the face of the flanker, who studied me through deep-set eyes that seemed to disappear into the darkness of his oversize black plastic helmet with a gold stripe down the seam.

Our heads seemed no more than a yard apart, and I could hear his words distinctly even though he was trying to whisper: "Look, kid, I'm going to crack back on you. Go down when I hit you. I don't want to hurt you, but I will if you don't go down. It's up to you." I didn't know if I should thank him or feel enraged. Did he think that I couldn't take care of myself? After all, he wasn't *that* much bigger and I wasn't that intimidated. Maybe he was seven years older, but what did that mean out here on the football field? This wasn't Iwo Jima.

"Ready! Set!" The quarterback was up under the center, checking the alignment and barking cadence. "One ... two ..." The snap came back, and it was a quick pitch to the tailback around my end. The flanker with the whiskers came in low, and I rattled the side of his helmet with a glancing shot from my left forearm. He seemed startled, but he held his block until the tailback had broken free and the coach's whistle signaled the play dead.

"Look, kid," he repeated, no longer whispering. "I'm trying to save you a lot of grief. Don't make it hard for me."

The varsity again lined up over the ball, but this time the flanker went to the other side. "Ready! Set! One ... two ... three ..." It was a trap up the middle, and the fierce rattling of the shoulder pads and the crunch of the helmets testified to the brutality of the contact.

"Oh! Oh, my God ... Oh!" The screams came from the point of attack ... and there, lying on his back, his white jersey stained with crimson, was the freshman middle guard, a big farm boy from Iowa, writhing in agony, his hands clawing at his face. "Oh, my God!" he cried over and over.

His nose was shattered—in those days nobody wore face guards—and some of his splintered teeth hung from his bloody lips. A thick-necked varsity lineman danced over the freshman and shouted: "Welcome to college football, kid! We know you're going to love it! It'll just take a little getting used to, that's all." Some of the others laughed. The coaches seemed not to notice. They summoned two student managers from the sidelines to remove the freshman, and then play continued.

Suddenly I felt sick, as if I might vomit right there on the field. Was this college football? Was this how it was played? Didn't anybody care that the boy from Iowa had been disfigured?

"Ready! Set!"

The flanker was off my left shoulder again, breathing heavily, squinting quizzically at me. "Don't make it hard for me, kid. Or for you."

"One . . . two . . ." The tailback had the ball again, slanting outside behind the fullback. The flanker cut into my thighs, easier than before, as if to test my resistance. I went down softly and he fell on top of me. "Thanks," he said simply. "I'm glad you understand."

* * * * *

The first play of any game always is the worst—as you test yourself in that initial struggle for supremacy over your opponent. It had been that way in high school for me, and it would be that way in college too. We were in our freshman game uniforms, which were hand-me-downs from the varsity, tattered gold shirts that had been patched and pants that had been laundered so many times that they appeared more white than gold. The dressing room for this opening game had been ghostly quiet as the coaches circulated among us and, for the first time, really seemed to recognize us as people, as apprehensive young men who were about to enter the arena for our baptism under fire.

"You feeling OK? Good, good. It's normal to be nervous the first time. But you'll be OK. Just do it like it's practice."

Out on the sun-lit field the University of Kansas freshmen already were exercising, looking better than we looked, I thought, in what seemed to be sparkling new uniforms of white, red, and silver. We kicked off to them, and it was baptism time.

I was at left end, on the open side of the field, when the flanker split from the huddle first and positioned himself three yards to my left. The fullback was in the slot, and the tailback was all alone behind the quarterback.

"One . . . two . . ."

It was a basic play, a quick pitch to the tailback on the outside. The flanker flailed at my legs, grunting and gasping. I tried to fend him off with my left arm while I followed the fullback who was boring at me as the primary blocker. He was standing straight up but then he dipped, and as I went down to meet his charge head on, he banged his elbow directly into my mouth . . . and I could feel the tissue tear and taste the blood. He had hung one on me, and as I toppled beneath a pile of bodies, I wanted desperately to thrust my tongue forward to check my teeth. Were they still in place? Or would I find some of them on the ground? The front of my mouth was numb, without any feeling. I rolled over and slowly put my right hand to my mouth. Thank God, I still had my teeth.

I didn't want to get back up and play. I wanted to hurry to the sidelines and tell somebody they didn't do it like this in high school, that they didn't purposely try to knock out teeth, that this wasn't what I had bargained for. But I didn't—because Kansas was lining up and getting ready to run at me again. The flanker was there on the outside and the fullback was in the slot, looking even more violent.

"One . . . two . . ."

* * * * *

Spring practice began in the raw winds of March and ended in the gentle breezes of May. It was the worst experience of my life because spring practice, unlike the fall season, had no games to break the routine . . . and the constant pounding and hacking. Yes, we played intrasquad games every Saturday, but they weren't real games. If a coach didn't like what he saw, he stopped everything and ran it again, like a movie director.

Through the wind sprints of winter in the field house to the early, seemingly endless blocking sessions indoors, I had discovered in my heart, if not yet in my mind, that this wasn't what I wanted to do for the next four years. But it was a black secret that I carried around inside me. How could I quit? No, of course, quitting was out of the question. I couldn't let down those who had sent me off with their cheers and great expectations. No, I would make it . . . and they would be proud of me. Nobody else felt the way I felt, and I simply would have to change my outlook.

Spring practice started on an unaccustomed note of levity. Two nonscholarship players appeared, under-weight-looking kids whose names nobody knew, not even the coaches. But for amusement, the coaches let them remain for a while, and they became almost like cheerleaders, jumping along the sidelines during practice games and, afterward, dashing around the dressing room, slapping bare backsides, and telling us how great we were.

It was as if they had rehearsed their routines. "Isn't it exciting to be a college football player?" one would say. And the other would respond: "Yes, and we're going to have a championship team. I just know we are."

My locker was next to the locker inhabited by a weight lifter from St. Louis, a kid who had been an all-American tackle in high school and who had been expected to move right into the varsity lineup as a college sophomore. It was obvious that he wasn't as excited about the whole business as the two non-scholarship players, and once, as they danced around us, he had rolled his eyes with a kind of resignation that seemed to ask: What are we doing here? Those guys are crazy and the rest of them are killers.

One of the two players had tried to lead a cheer right in the dressing cubicle, and the tackle finally had confronted him.

"Look, go away and leave us alone."

The nonscholarship player had seemed surprised. "If you don't like football, what are you doing here?" he had asked.

"I'm here because I'm paid to be here, that's why. Now get lost."

The two players had left, and a day or two later they were gone for good. The coaches finally had tired of their antics and had taken away their practice gear, suggesting firmly that "you'll get hurt if you don't leave now."

The hometown newspaper had dispatched the

sports editor to interview me, but he talked more than I did.

"How's it going? Great, I'll bet. Just great."

"Well, it's a little different than I—"

"They tell me you're doing just great. The folks at home ask about you all the time. That's why we're doing this story. You're gonna be starting on offense next fall, aren't you?"

"Well, eh—"

"Sure you are. Not many hands like yours around."

I had wanted to run away and hide, but I didn't—because I couldn't. There was nowhere to go—nowhere far enough away to hide the guilt and shame that welled up within me. In less than a year I had gone from a smiling, happy teenager to somebody who seldom found humor or joy in any part of life. At eighteen I was failing—for the first time in my life—and letting down those who had counted on me. As I shaved one afternoon before R.O.T.C. inspection, I asked the face in the mirror, "What's wrong with you?" And the face answered, "I'm a failure."

Pop drove the thirty miles from Jefferson City to Columbia every Saturday for the practice games, but we seldom talked about what caused the lump in my throat. How could I discuss it with him? He would be disappointed in me, too—if he knew. So I played the game with him.

"You doing all right?" he would ask.

"Sure, why do you ask?" I would say.

"Well, I was just wondering. You don't seem happy."

"If people beat on you every day, you wouldn't seem happy, either." And I had forced a laugh, and

64

Pop had forced a laugh, and then we talked about the weather.

The final spring game was a real game—for blood—and it matched the Golds against the Whites . . . our last chance to get in our licks and impress the coaches before we broke for the summer. The Golds ran at me on the very first play, and I fought off a blocker and tackled the ball carrier for a loss. They tried me again, and I ran the halfback out of bounds after two yards.

"I want him out of there!" one of the Gold coaches screamed, pointing at me. "I want that end on his back. I want that play to go. Get him out of there!"

On the next play they got me out of there. I went down in the pile and for a long time I didn't get up. Then I limped off and didn't come back. I should have been sad, I told myself, but I wasn't. Secretly I was rejoicing. After the game, as I sat in my cubicle and unlaced my shoulder pads, I told myself: This is the last time I'll ever wear any of this stuff. It's all over. I quit.

I was as big as many of them, and I was faster than most of them. I could catch better than any of them. But I just didn't have the heart—or the stomach—for it.

* * * * *

For me, football was in the past, but the residue of what I perceived as failure stayed with me, like a storm cloud, never far out of my consciousness. I had been a fair-haired boy, popular, successful, and everything I wanted had come so easily for me: letters in all sports, captain of the football team, student body president, National Honor Society, as many dates as I could handle. Now, at age eighteen, all of that was behind me. I had failed . . . had let down my friends—and my family. But most of all, I had let down myself. I hadn't been good enough and, even worse, I hadn't really wanted to be good enough. My mind told me that quitting had been a rational decision and a mark of courage. But my stomach told me something else: I was a quitter . . . and maybe even a coward.

My whole identity and sense of esteem had been constructed around my image as an athlete. Now that I wasn't an athlete anymore, what was I? Who was I? Would I ever be worth anything? Would anybody ever accept me again? Would anybody ever forgive me for what I had done? The football experience contaminated every crevice of my existence. I hadn't just failed as a football player: I had failed as a human being.

What would Pop say? How disappointed would he be with me? In early summer I finally mustered up the strength to share my decision with him. I flinched and said: "Pop, I'm not going to play football anymore. It's not worth it."

I had anticipated that he would ask how I could do this to him, but he didn't. Instead, he said, "Have you really thought it over?"

"Yes . . . I have."

"Well, that's fine then. I want you to do what you think is best. It's a decision nobody else can make. We're behind you—your mom and I—all the way."

I kept waiting for him to say more, but he didn't. And he never did. If he was disappointed, he never let me know it. And neither did Mom.

How would I answer my friends when they asked why I had quit? The strange thing was that nobody asked. That should have told me something, but it didn't.

* * * * *

She was pretty, self-confident, and popular, a high school senior who worked after school but who still found time to be socially active and an honor student. I was a college sophomore, majoring in journalism and guarding my dark secret with all the sophistication I could command. I'm not sure that others ever suspected the load of torment that I carried on my back and in my heart. If they had suspected, they would have been dumbfounded. I can see that now. To them, I still was the same person I'd always been, but in my mind I was different. When they reacted to me as they always had, I wanted to lash out at them as hypocrites, as people who weren't honest enough to treat me as the failure I was. It was all in my mind—I can see that so clearly now—but back then it was so very real to me.

Verna treated me not like a failure but as if I mattered, and I hung on to her as if my life depended on it, which it did, symbolically, at least. We dated steadily, and the red flags were ignored by both of us, the unreasonable, self-centered demands that we made on each other.

She pressured me to give up semipro baseball so I wouldn't be out of town so much; I quit playing baseball. I pressured her to marry me and not be concerned about finishing four years of college; she agreed. I was certain that if she didn't marry me, I was doomed to loneliness for the rest of my life. After all,

I was nobody, and surely only she ever would accept me as a lifetime partner.

*****

When you think you're nobody, you can't ever stop running, and not even a wife and children can slow you down. At the newspaper office in Jefferson City, where I started as sports editor and later was reporter, city editor, and managing editor, I stumbled upon one of life's bizarre truths: If you work hard enough and long enough, you can camouflage the internal garbage that pollutes your life. You don't get rid of it, but you relegate it to the depths of your soul, and it seldom bubbles to the surface if you stay in your own little pond and splash around like the big fish that you desperately want yourself and others to believe you are.

The penalty that you pay for this trickery is that, away from your little pond, everybody and everything become a threat. Other writers seem more imaginative than you do. Other editors seem more on top of things than you do. Other newspapers look livelier than your newspaper. I could talk to a high school journalism class and charm the kids right out of their socks. Who were they to challenge me? But if I went to a state press meeting and the guys from St. Louis and Kansas City were there, I found someplace to hide. Obviously, they were smart enough to unmask me for what I really was—somebody who wasn't good enough to make it when and where it counted. It was all nonsense, of course, but if you're young enough and frightened enough, you believe it. And if you believe it, it's true.

*****

I worked six days every week and three or four

nights, because I also broadcast sports for the newspaper-owned radio station. When Verna complained that she felt neglected and left out of my life, I told her that she was shortsighted and selfish and that eventually, when I made it big, she'd be sorry that she had behaved as an anchor. She responded by mothering Jay and Grant more and being a wife to me less. It should have been another red flag that we both recognized and acted upon, but it wasn't. It was a pattern from which we never escaped—and ultimately it chewed at our feelings for each other and hounded the marriage until the marriage was dead.

One of these days, I knew, I was going to be an editor—if not in Louisville, then somewhere else. And when that happened, it would be undeniable evidence to everybody that I wasn't a failure, that I wasn't like my father, that others couldn't run over me and make me dance to their music. Conversely, if I didn't make it as an editor on some newspaper in some city, it would be undeniable evidence to everybody that I didn't have what it took, that I was . . . nobody. I decided that everything had to be channeled into becoming an editor and succeeding as an editor—and the marriage and Jay and Grant would have to take a seat way in the back until then. Later on, there would be plenty of time to make amends and to do what I now had no time or inclination to do. Tomorrow, I said to them, things would be different. But tomorrow never arrived—not even after the telephone call that came during a March snowstorm and enabled me to sell myself to *The Charlotte News* as managing editor.

I had written a flurry of letters applying for jobs

because I saw the handwriting on the wall in Louisville. When the old-time city editor retired, I expected to succeed him, but the job went to somebody else. I was to become assistant editor in the Sunday department, and when they told me, I felt as if the sky had collapsed. The message was plain to me: I wasn't good enough. And from the closets of my past the skeletons danced gleefully. I cried through a sleepless night, and the next morning I still hurt, but my anger was blotting out the pain.

How could they do this to me? Because I was wounded it never occurred to me that somebody else might make a better city editor. In my fury I decided that I would go into the Sunday department, all right, but I would stay there only until I had found somebody who recognized my ability for what it was worth. Verna didn't object to the move to North Carolina because by then she knew it was futile to object because I tended to tune out what I didn't want to hear. Pop objected not directly but by raising a question: "Why? How do you know things will be better there?" I answered by telling him that I knew because I would make things better.

In the spring we set out for North Carolina, and Jay, as we drove along in the station wagon, asked, "Daddy, when we get there, will we be happy?"

I patted him on the leg and assured him that, yes, we would be happy. And we were, relatively, for a few years as my career prospered and as I came to understand in my stomach as well as in my head that I was a winner. I was good at what I was doing; I knew it and others knew it, too. At long last the ghosts were put to rest, and I realized that the good feeling that I'd had about myself as a child wasn't dead. It simply had been buried for so many years. Now it was alive and kicking—and so was I, although the marriage was shriveling. I didn't think much about it. If Verna did, she never confronted me with it. Instead, she retreated more heavily into mothering and more deeply into religion.

It was as if I had two lives—one at work from which I got my sustenance and one at home from which I got . . . well, I wasn't exactly sure about that.

What had happened to me personally? How could I be so satisfied at work when my homelife was crumbling? As I look back, I believe that professionally I had become a prime example of the theory that if people can find one thing in which they are accepted and in which they excel, they can gain from it an energy that influences other areas of their lives. An airplane stunt pilot, Jim Holland, who always seemed supremely confident in everything he did, once told me that the color of his whole life had changed when he realized that in an airplane he could do things that virtually nobody else even would attempt. If that hadn't happened, he said, he probably would have spent the rest of his life pumping gasoline on a street corner somewhere—and hating himself. Years later Stanford University psychologist Philip Zimbardo would agree: Yes, it was possible to quiet the skeletons and the ghosts by mastering a single skill, especially if the skill was people-related.

Why didn't the energy wash over into my marriage? Why didn't all parts of my life come together? I'm afraid that the damage already had been done inside our hearts and minds. Tragically, it was irreversible damage—not because it couldn't have been fixed but because neither of us talked about the need to fix it. We went through the motions of living and somehow convinced ourselves that it was real.

I was on my way to becoming an executive editor of a newspaper that over the years I would help shape into what I thought a responsible and lively afternoon newspaper ought to be. It should have been smooth sailing for me and my family. But it wasn't—because I uncovered another one of life's bizarre truths: the more you like yourself and the more you succeed, the more you demand from life. I wasn't getting what I wanted and needed from the marriage—and I hadn't for a long, long time. When I felt that I didn't deserve anything better, I accepted it the way it was. But now that my feelings had changed, I was aware of what I was missing, and I was miserable. But I didn't know what to do about it.

In many ways Jay and Grant had become strangers to me. I didn't know what to do about that either.

Chapter 5

With the Children, Good Times and Bad

The toe of the pilot's black boot nudged against my left hip—our prearranged signal that the fun was about to begin—and over the radio two voices cracked into my ears through the receivers inside my sheepskin-lined helmet.

"Ah . . . OK, Mike, you ready?"

"Roger, Jim, ah, I think it's time."

I turned my head to the right and studied the green-and-white airplane that was flying alongside us, our wing tips seeming almost to touch. There was no way I could talk back to the pilot because I had no speaker, and neither did Grant, my teenage son, who hunched in the front seat of the other airplane and smiled tentatively at me. I lifted my gloved right hand, raised my thumb and waggled it toward Grant. Immediately he returned the signal and his smile broadened. He was ready. Now I waggled my thumb over my right shoulder so the pilot in the seat behind me could see it. Instantly the black control stick between my legs popped forward, as if shoved by an invisible hand, and the 200-horsepower engine of our red-and-white checkerboard airplane growled angrily. The nose fell quickly and the airspeed indicator told me that this dive was much steeper than any of the others . . . 120 . . . 140 . . . 160 . . . 180 . . . 200. Then back came the stick, toward my stomach, and we pulled out of the dive as pressure equal to six times the force of gravity jammed me down hard into my seat, pried open my mouth, and clawed the skin away from my eyes. Now the nose was pointed straight toward heaven, and the throttle was wide open. Incredibly, this 19-foot-long airplane, the world's best for stunting, was climbing at a 90-degree angle away from the red South Carolina clay that stretched out 2,500 feet below us.

The control stick whipped to the left so abruptly that it banged into the inside of my thigh. This caused the airplane to begin a counterclockwise spin as we went up. Frantically, I tried to find a landmark—some piece of cloud or ground—so that I could count the spins, but I couldn't find anything . . . not even Grant's airplane. Oh, yes, there it was, a blur of green and white, over to the right . . . now to the left . . . now . . . where did it go? I'd lost it. I'd lost everything. Mercy, now I was lost, unable to distinguish between nose up and nose down. Were we still spinning? I wasn't even sure of that.

But no matter where we were, one thing was obvious: Despite full power, the airplane was beginning to stall, unable to maintain its speed because of the drastic angle of the climb. The engine continued to roar, but now the airplane had stopped its ascent. We hung in space for a split second and then we began to fall back, tail down, in a slow spin caused by the torque of the engine. Now we were tumbling, tail over nose, and each time we flipped over I had the heart-stopping sensation that I was being squeezed out of the airplane, thrown over the trailing edge of the top wing, beneath which I cried out in agony as I wedged my knees under the instrument panel.

Flip . . . flop . . . flip. We continued to tumble, and through the haze of disorientation the pilot's voice burned into my ears: "OK, hey, look off your right shoulder."

Which shoulder was my right? Oh, there it was . . . but what was out there? Unbelievably, it was the green-and-white airplane, tumbling along with us, in graceful slow motion, smooth and controlled, not tumbling awkwardly as we seemed to be.

Then it was gone and over the top of the wing, as we plummeted, I alternately saw blue sky and red clay. But even as disoriented as I was, I was able to establish that while the sky seemed riveted into position, the clay unmistakably was rushing toward us . . . and I flashed back to a hurried preflight conversation with my pilot: "Everything is rehearsed and planned to the nth degree. I never feel there's chance involved with anything I do. I'm flying the ultimate airplane for stunting, and there's nothing it can't recover from—except starting a maneuver too close to the ground."

At that instant I desperately wished he hadn't told me that. Then, suddenly, the tumbling stopped, and we split out of the dive, so close to the ground that I thought I could recognize the cones on the pine trees.

"What happened?" The voice on the radio sounded urgent, puzzled, even angry.

My pilot's voice was level and routine: "Ah, Jim, I was getting a little low . . . and I didn't want to try it. How 'bout if we go again? Passengers, you up to it?"

* * * * *

That remarkable afternoon in the airplane was a benchmark of the relationship that I had with Grant, the second-born son, who was then fifteen and who, on the one hand, wanted to keep his distance from me but who, on the other hand, seemed to relish, as much as I did, the closeness that we both felt on our many special occasions.

The airplane ride was one of the most special occasions that we ever shared, and it had come about simply because he asked to do it. On television I had seen an advertisement for Carowinds, the giant theme park that straddles the border between North Carolina and South Carolina. The advertisement had featured film footage of a pilot spinning, looping, and tumbling a tiny airplane, doing stunts that seemed to defy the laws of possibility. It was to promote the park's daily air shows by two veteran stunt pilots, Jim Holland, who had been decorated by England for heroism during World War II, and Lindsay (Mike) Hess, a former opera singer whose air sense enabled him to fly by feel and sound, without paying undue attention to the instruments.

Would one of them take me for a ride sometime so that I could write a story about it for my newspaper? Yes, certainly, they would be delighted. And so on a partly cloudy, 52-degree day in March I had met Hess, and we had flown in his Pitts Special, a two-wing, 1,100-pound stunt airplane that is made half of tubular steel and half of spruce wood and that is covered with a treated fabric that is stretched taut against the frame.

There were only about a hundred of them in the world, Hess said, $31,000 airplanes that were handmade in two months at the Curtis Pitts factory in Afton, Wyoming. Hess had put his year-old Pitts Special through every maneuver in the books with me in the front seat, and I had gotten so nauseated that I quickly had filled the air-sickness bag that Hess thoughtfully had taped to the instrument panel. It was both an awful and an exhilarating experience, and I had shared it with Grant as we sat in the backyard on a sunny afternoon and watched the fluffy white clouds drift south above the towering pine trees that the two of us had spent part of a summer trimming with our saw and ax.

"Gosh, you're lucky," Grant said.

"Why?"

"Well, you get to do a lot of interesting things. How many people ever fly in a stunt plane? Boy, would I like to do that sometime."

"Well, maybe we could arrange it. What do you think?"

The size of Grant's eyes told me what he thought. He was ready—as he always seemed to be—to get going, to taste the unusual, to try something new and exciting.

I called Hess, the pilot, the next day and asked if another flight would be possible.

"Sure, whenever you want. But you told me you have two sons. What about the other one? Doesn't he want to go, too?"

"You know, I didn't ask him. But I will."

Jay, the firstborn son, then was sixteen, and I knew what his answer would be—a polite "no" and a questioning stare that seemed to say, I don't know why anybody would want to fly in a little airplane and get sick.

So Grant and I had flown and then, at dinner, we had shared our excitement with Jay, who seemed mildly disinterested but also wistful: "You two do some crazy things together."

Yes, Grant and I had done the crazy and the not-so-crazy, the things that cushion a relationship against the hard times of adolescence, when a child's need to assert independence often fuzzes the inclination to be part of the family.

As a Little League pitcher, Grant had idolized Bob Gibson, the Cardinals' fire-baller, after whom he had wanted to pattern his pitching motion. One year I had written a letter to Gibson and addressed it simply to him at Busch Memorial Stadium, the home of the Cardinals, in St. Louis. In the letter I had explained Grant's admiration for him, and I had asked if Gibson would be kind enough to autograph a picture and mail it to Grant. In four weeks the picture had arrived, not merely signed but with this handwritten message: "To Grant, from another pitcher. Best of luck, Bob Gibson."

Not long after that we had been in St. Louis—Jay, Grant, their mother, and I—and I had arranged with the Cardinals for Grant and me to sit in the dugout before a game with the San Diego Padres and visit with the players. Did Jay want to come with us? No, he wasn't interested in meeting any baseball players, he said—and so Grant and I, alone, were in the dugout, along with Dal Maxvil, Jose Cruz, Joe Torre, Ted Sizemore, Lou Brock . . . and Bob Gibson.

"Gosh, you'll never know how much this means to me," Grant said.

"Yes, I *do* know," I said. "I know how I'd have felt about it when I was your age."

In contrast, Jay and I had done together very few crazy and not-so-crazy things. Jay had joined Grant and me in erecting a basketball goal beside the driveway in front of the house, but he had not wanted to play.

"Why not?" I wanted to know.

"Because I think it's kind of silly—bouncing a ball around and trying to shoot it through a hoop."

He had started to go inside to read, but I had intercepted him and insisted that he shoot baskets.

"I don't want to."

"Well, you're going to. Just dribble the ball up to the basket and shoot it. Just make one, and you can go inside or do anything you want."

"I don't want to—and you have no right to make me."

"Quit talking and shoot the ball. Just make one."

For a quarter of an hour Jay bounced the ball and shot it wildly off the backboard, often missing the rim entirely, not because he *couldn't* do it but because he *wouldn't* do it.

"Jay, you're behaving like a kid!"

"I *am* a kid."

Grant had laughed, but I had not. There seemed no two ways about it: Jay was going to do things his way—and his mother's way. And it had set up what seemed to be a classic confrontation that so often

79

developed—Jay and his mother against Grant and me.

I found some comfort in something I had read: Adolescence can be a strained time and about the best thing that parents can do is ride it out with the knowledge that what their child is going through probably is normal. At some point healthy children with healthy parents get their act together and relate to both parents in appropriate ways.

Adolescence, as we all know, is a tough time for everybody. Teenagers form the only age group in which the death rate is increasing—because of suicides. Infant mortality is down; the geriatric group is living longer; but more adolescents are dying.

Why? There are a host of reasons, and you almost can take your pick. It's a painful period as adolescents struggle to separate from childhood and move into adulthood—even as they long to keep the trappings of childhood, which includes parents who are omnipotent. The adolescent has to make the parents not omnipotent and take on the responsibilities of adulthood, which is a tall order.

Adolescents tend to look at their parents hypercritically. They try not to like most things about them even as they love most things about them—if the parents are reasonably dedicated to parenting. There is a period when an adolescent looks for gender identity. "Am I a boy or a girl?" the adolescent asks. "Who am I and what do I want to be? After whom do I want to model myself?" It's at this point that the attachment to parents can be and often is confusing.

The confusion seems to hinge on the reality that as children become sexual, they normally are attracted to the parent of the opposite sex. If you're a believer in Freudian principles, you think that a boy is in love with his mother and angry with his father because he can't have her. But eventually the boy breaks away from the mother because sexual attraction toward her tends to fade as he matures and is replaced by appropriate esteem for both parents.

Yes, that's what all the books said, I reflected. But when was it going to happen in our family, with Jay? It had never been so much of a problem with Grant, who, through thick and thin, always acknowledged my presence even though he was baffled by my work habits. He sometimes made fun of my long hours, but the implication was: If that's what makes *you* happy, go right ahead.

The thought that my relationship with Jay might never mature into anything stronger turned my hands wet and cold and inverted my stomach. After all, the books said that the coming together of parents and children was possible only if parents were reasonably dedicated to parenting. Maybe I was striking out with Jay because I wasn't reasonable, and perhaps this had caused him to doubt that I was dedicated. That little session in the driveway with the basketball surely wasn't reasonable. No, I had been off base, and I would acknowledge that to Jay and tell him that I was sorry.

Although we often clashed and he went his way and I went mine, Jay and I strangely had a years-long history of being able to talk about what was on our minds. There had been the time, around Thanksgiving of his thirteenth year, when the two of us had stretched out across his bed and talked as if we had lost all track of time, which we had.

"Jay, if you rated me as a father on a scale of zero to ten, how would I stack up?"

"About eight. I think you're fair with me most of the time, and you take an interest in a lot of things and you work hard around the house and in the yard. I hear other kids talk about their fathers, and some of them say pretty bad things. I couldn't do that. I think I'm lucky to live here."

"What do you dislike about me?"

"You come home from work in a bad mood sometimes, and you yell at me and get mad when I'm doing things that don't make you mad when you're not in a bad mood. You cuss too much when you're mad. Your business is words, and it seems to me you could find some better words to use."

I asked Jay if it scared him when I yelled.

"Yes, sometimes it does. I can tell as soon as you get home if you're in a bad mood or a good mood. I can tell by how hard your heels hit the floor when you walk in the house and by how long you stand in the kitchen and talk with Mommy—and by how soon you pour yourself a drink. I wish you wouldn't yell. There has to be a better way. A trainer makes his lions perform out of fear. He'd get better results if they performed out of love."

I asked Jay if he thought I was disappointed in him because he displayed no interest in sports, which were so important to Grant and me.

"Well, since you asked, there have been times when I've felt that you were a little disappointed. You and Grant play ball and watch the games on television, and sometimes I feel like an outsider. No, not really an outsider. What I mean is that sometimes you seem to think that the games on television are the most important things to you."

I flinched . . . because he had nailed me with his honesty, and he knew it. He continued pounding in the nail, not because he wanted to hurt me but because we had agreed to share what was on our minds.

"I don't think most adults are happy. I don't think you're happy as much as you have a right to be. It seems to me that most men, like you, are too busy, tied down with their work. Do you know that we hardly ever take a vacation? Oh, maybe we go to the beach for a few days, but we hardly ever take a real vacation. I mean I wish we could go away for a long time—like maybe a month. When I see people work such long hours, like you, I have to wonder if it's worth it. Is any job worth it? I believe that I'd wonder if I were suited for my job if I had to work hours like that. Why do you do it?"

Well, I thought, there's a time for honesty, all right, but this is going too far. How could I tell Jay why I worked so long and hard? How could I explain that I was running frantically to succeed, because I didn't want to fail, because I didn't want anybody ever to be in a position to turn the screws on me as so many had done to my father? How could I tell him that workaholism is the only sickness that society applauds under the misnomer of "dedication" to career? How could I tell him that spending hours and hours at the office was a socially sanctioned way to avoid spending time with his mother, from whom I was becoming more and more distant?

So I fudged on Jay and instead of total honesty I delivered partial honesty. What did it matter if I didn't tell him *everything?* After all, a young boy probably couldn't understand it anyway.

"Jay, people who are serious about their careers have to work long and hard—longer and harder than everybody else. We do it because it's expected of us. It's the price that business extracts from people on the way up. I work every Saturday because every editor in this newspaper's history has worked on Saturdays. That's the way it is. I knew the price when I bought into it."

I told Jay that in the wonderful world of big business it wasn't uncommon for the boss to call a Sunday afternoon meeting and to expect everybody to be there—regardless of what had been planned. If you analyzed what caused the necessity of a Sunday meeting, you couldn't find anything, but if you said that you couldn't come because it was your son's birthday and you were having a party, then your loyalty was judged to be misplaced. The sad fact of business life, I said, was that it forced many of us to bend when we wanted to stand tall.

Jay's expression was a mixture of amusement and confusion. "Then why do you do it?"

"We do it because it's expected of us," I repeated. "I wish I could explain it better, but I can't."

So much for candor.

* * * * *

How much time does it take to be a reasonably dedicated parent? Is it so vast that it means that good parenting and serious-minded pursuit of career are incompatible? Does it have to be either/or? Can't it be both?

There are those who agree with neurosurgeon Norman Shealy, who with his wife wrote the book *To Parent or Not?* and who told me that parenting doesn't interfere with "healthy" striving toward career success. "But we're not talking usually about healthy striving. We're talking about what white males tend to make out of their careers. In our society there has been a tremendous tendency in the last thirty or forty years for families to be torn asunder by careers—especially with fathers feeling the need to work more than eight or ten hours a day, with fathers feeling the need to move frequently . . . and uprooting their families in the process. It's impossible to combine parenthood with that kind of behavior," but, Shealy said, the pursuit of career can be more reasonable and, when it is, parenting can fit right in with it. After all, "the time that children require is limited . . . and it's possible to have the best of both. But is it hard? Yes, it's hard—and it requires some effort, as all worthwhile things do."

There are those who dismiss that as a simplistic approach and who believe, like psychologist Maurice Prout, that one—either parenting or career—must take a toll on the other and that it's impossible to have the very best of both.

The price of good parenting can be high, he said, as can the price of inadequate parenting. "If you're going to spend time with the kids, you have to give up your goal of being chairman of the department by the time you're forty. You're not going to work as hard, and even if you try, you still need to be home for dinner by seven." On the other hand, he said, if a parent doesn't back off from work commitment and turn much energy toward the children, there builds a vacuum that eventually extracts a price in terms of the children's ability to function in a normal, healthy way.

What it amounts to is choosing your loss. If it's career, the loss is immediate because ambitions necessarily must be bridled. If it's parenting, then the loss comes later. When the children are in their teens—or even in early adulthood—there is a sense of distance, of acting out. You talk with a friend about his relationship with his children, and you sense that you don't have it. Why not? Because you weren't there.

Why are parents today not as successful in general as they might be? For one thing the culture doesn't put parenting first anymore. It puts something else first—personal success, growth, or fulfillment. The example of intimacy is not there for the children, who suffer because it's not possible to grow and be successful without being able to be intimate. That's why we not so infrequently read about successful people who commit suicide at the apex of their careers. They seem to have everything, but in reality they have very little . . . or nothing.

Realistically, how good is it possible to be as a parent? There are some who feel that the nature of effective parenting doesn't permit greatness, but every one of us can move toward being a "good enough" parent.

It's not terribly difficult, we're told, to be a "good enough" parent. The skills are the same as we use in other endeavors—the ability to hear what the other person is saying and to empathize with that person, to set limits, to grasp another's value system and filter it through your own and come to personal principles that stand—as opposed to taking polls and figuring out what will fly today.

The "good enough" parent is the best kind of parent it's possible to be. Nobody can be more because of the extremely fine line that must be walked between frustration and gratification. The "good enough" parent is able to frustrate the children—by setting limits—to the point that the children move against the parent. Yet the children must be gratified enough by the relationship to be able to move against the parent without feeling guilty, to push off and know that the parent is still going to be there and love them, no matter what.

Above all else, the children need to know that they are loved by the parents, loved consistently and uniformly even though the parents may not approve of what the children do or how they do it. The children must know that they will be loved no more if they succeed gloriously, no less if they fail dismally. It is this and everything that comes before and after that make parenting so very difficult for so many of us so much of the time. We are being asked to do what we have not been trained to do—and we are told that the stakes virtually are the life or death of our children.

Is it any wonder that when our children are born, many of us, as I was, are torn between the ecstasy of the miracle and the somberness of the burden? We know that the name of the game is emotional communication—making the time we have with our children count by hearing what they say and by responding appropriately to it. It sounds easier than it is. I once asked therapist Bill Bruce if it's possible to be a "good enough" parent if you not infrequently come home from work physically and mentally spent and wanting not dialogue but solitude. Bruce's answer:

"You have to ask what kind of life you're leading. Why are you permitting yourself to do this? If a job takes this much out of you, then something is wrong with the job and something is wrong inside you. If society sets up jobs that kill people, what does this say about us? Is this any different from working in a coal mine without any safety devices?"

* * * * *

The St. Louis-San Diego baseball game was fifteen minutes away from its start, and Grant's autograph book rapidly was being filled. It was time to leave, and Grant and I walked down the concrete runway that led away from the dugout. Off to the left, sitting quietly by himself, staring at the floor, was Ted Simmons, the all-star catcher.

"Hey, look who's there," Grant whispered excitedly.

"He looks like he might be meditating," I said.

"Can we get his autograph?" Grant asked.

"Yes, that's why we're here. Go ahead and ask him."

"I think I'd feel better if you asked. Will you?"

I approached Simmons with Grant's book and my pen, and before I said anything he looked up, nodded, reached mechanically for the book and pen, and signed his name. Then he again focused his eyes on the floor.

"He *is* meditating," Grant said. "I'm sure he is."

Well, I told Grant, you ought to know because, after all, the two of us did pay our money and go through the transcendental meditation program together. It was yet another of the many threads that laced us together. Jay had not wanted to join us in the program, and his mother insisted that it was not something with which he would feel comfortable.

Yet as Grant and I stormed home nightly from our lessons and shared enthusiastically what we felt and thought, Jay impressed me as a boy who was standing on the outside with his nose pressed against the window and yearning to be asked to come in, despite his protestations that he was happy where he was.

Now, with the first pitch only minutes away, Grant and I wound our way through the stands at Busch Memorial Stadium and to the seats in which Jay and his mother sat, talking quietly.

"Hey, Jay," Grant began, "you wouldn't believe the people I just saw and talked to."

"Well, you were gone a long time. I thought maybe you'd gotten lost." Jay handed Grant a box of popcorn and looked straight at me. In his eyes I read an unmistakable message of pain: You don't even know who I am, do you?

Chapter 6

Rumbles of Discontent: The Mid-Life Crisis

This was the one speech I wanted to make above all others, and I had leaped at the invitation to come to Phoenix, Arizona, for the annual meeting of Associated Press Managing Editors, the professional organization to which I had belonged when I was an editor and of which I once was a member of the board of directors. Would I discuss with them why I had left an editorship and gone back to full-time writing? Surely, other editors would want to know. Did I ever regret my decision? Or did I consider it a new lease on life? Would I talk candidly about the gut issues in my walking away from the kind of job to which I had aspired since boyhood?

The convention hall's 750 seats were occupied, and the latecomers were beginning to jam up against the walls along the sides and in the back. It was late afternoon on the last day of the week-long convention, and the chairman of this segment of the program leaned away from the walnut podium and whispered that I must have a lot of friends out there, people who would surrender their time on the sun-drenched tennis courts to listen to me talk.

The chairman rapped for attention, which promptly was given, and then he introduced me as somebody who had said that leaving an editorship at *The Charlotte News* and becoming a columnist for *The Philadelphia Inquirer* was "like dying and going to heaven." They laughed, and I was pleased—because it well might be the last time that laughter would be appropriate. What I was going to say wouldn't be funny.

Now I was up in front of the editors—and many wives, too—and telling them how good it was to see so many of my old colleagues again.

"In the novel *Dubin's Lives*," I began, "the main character cries out that he wants to live a hundred lives because one is not enough. Well, the fact is that none of us can have a hundred lives. For most of us, one life is all we have. I consider myself a fortunate exception because, you see, I'm living my second life at this very moment."

I last had seen most of the editors five years earlier when I mounted the platform at the convention in Williamsburg and introduced General William Westmoreland, Dr. Michael DeBakey, and Jill Wine Volner, who offered their perceptions of how they had been treated by the press. But only a few of the editors, my closest friends, had known that I was staggering on the ropes, an unhappy husband and a disillusioned editor—two months away from a separation that ended my marriage of twenty-two years, and eight months away from surrendering a job that I once thought I loved.

Why was I then so unhappy and disillusioned? I told them that I wasn't going to dwell on the marriage and why it failed, but I was going to talk about why I quit as an editor. It simply amounted to this: It wasn't fun anymore, and life is too short not to try to engage in some of the things that are fun.

To the editors I posed this question: Why did you go into the newspaper business? But then, without allowing time for reflection, I answered the question for them: Yes, of course, you wanted to write.

Never in my whole life, I told them, had I ever met anybody who came into the newspaper business because he wanted to wrestle with affirmative action reports, draft an annual budget, sign personnel evaluations, plan the company's United Way campaign. Yet when we become editors, these are the things that occupy our time, and we wonder why the zing has gone out of our lives. We have been seduced by money, power, prestige, recognition, an executive secretary, and color-coordinated draperies. Becoming an editor is something we *should* do if we want to stamp ourselves as successful in our profession. It is a normal progression for the best of us—to "move up" from writing to editing.

So the question then becomes: How does anybody walk away from all of that? How does anybody embrace what he thought he wanted and then turn it loose—when he discovers that it wasn't really what he wanted or what he thought it was? How does anybody let go of a dream without asking: "What's wrong with me?" We have what we thought we always wanted, but we're not satisfied. So we repeat the question: "What's wrong?"

Nobody stirred in the audience. Our eyes were locked in contact. The editors seemed in step with me, every single one of them.

I pushed back from my outline because the words

were coming so easily, and I suggested to the editors that the kind of disillusionment about which I was talking wasn't confined to the newspaper business. Everywhere these days, it seemed, disillusionment was rampant. I was going to share with them parts of a letter that had come to me just the other day, a letter handwritten on the personal stationery of the chairman of the board of a major New York corporation:

"I'm a middle-aged guy . . . and I guess you could say that I've been fairly successful from a business standpoint. I'm making far more money than I ever thought possible thirty years ago, when I got out of college. Yet I know for certain that this is only part of what life is all about. There has to be more to it than this. I feel so empty . . ."

Five years ago, I told the editors, as I stood on the convention platform in Williamsburg, I felt so empty, too. But now I feel so full—so full of contentment. The one thing that I had heard from so many of them during the week in Phoenix amounted to this: "Golly, you seem so satisfied that I really envy you. You look at peace." Yes, I said, I was going to explain why I was satisfied and peaceful, but first I wanted to explore some reasons why "success" was so empty to me—and why I suspected it was so empty to so many others, including more than a few in this very audience.

That brought a stir, a foot-shuffling, throat-clearing kind of restlessness that I had expected. Some of them were uncomfortable, but if the shoe fit . . .

I told them that age forty had been a turning point for me, an age that was so much more than one year beyond thirty-nine. Age forty is when those of us who are lucky begin to feel the sting of the burr under the saddle and wonder frantically where the hurt is coming from. Once I had interviewed a forty-seven-year-old psychiatrist who said that the hurt was from realizing, at long last, that life is finite, that time is beginning to run out on us, that if we didn't get 'em last year, we're probably not going to get 'em this year or next year. If we weren't happy last year, we're probably not going to be happy this year or next year.

Age forty is a time when we have to separate the impossible dreams from the possible dreams and turn loose of that which is impossible. If happiness is not possible in an editorship or in a marriage, then we need to recognize this as reality . . . and confront it. It hurts; oh, how it hurts. At times the pain can seem almost life-threatening, and it comes from what therapists call a "confrontation with discrepancy"—the gap between how we thought it was going to be when we planned our lives and how we now know it really is. This is when, like Peggy Lee, we cry out in our agony and ask, "Is that all there is?" It's when we are disillusioned if we don't win the Pulitzer Prize—or if we do . . . and realize that it's "just" the Pulitzer Prize.

It's the same thing with being an editor—or at least it was for me. It is this confrontation with discrepancy that causes some of us to drink too much, eat too much, cheat on our wives—and cheat ourselves, too, in the sense that we forfeit our right to enjoy life.

As I swept the audience with my eyes, I couldn't believe what was happening. Many of the editors were nodding in agreement. Yes, they understood the confrontation—and how much it hurt.

I asked them if they knew what had to be done to stop the pain. And then I told them that I thought a heavy dose of unadorned introspection was needed— with this as the jackpot question: What do I *really* want to do with my life?

We each, I said, have to define success for ourselves. But the problem is that so many of us permit society to define it for us. The price for that ultimately is pain and anxiety. I told them about an interview with New York psychiatrist Theodore Isaac Rubin, who had called the American culture "crazy" because it pushes people naked into the world and tells them that they can buy the self-esteem they need to survive if they will achieve, achieve, achieve. "But the result of this craziness," Rubin said, "is the disillusionment that comes with the realization, usually in mid-life, that no amount of success ever is enough and the slightest failure is too much. In keeping with our neuroticism, success and failure have nothing to do with what we achieve or fail to achieve—but with our expectations of ourselves. We have a compulsive need to make up the self-esteem that's not there. And that's not possible—with any amount of success. The slightest failure becomes attached to self-hate . . . Success that is based on hunger for self-esteem never brings the fulfillment that was hoped for, but since this hunger is the basic thrust for most Americans' climb for success, it's no wonder that we have become a nation plagued by depression, anxiety, and disillusionment . . . We fail when we succeed in our culture, and often when we succeed in self-realization, we fail in terms of our culture."

The clarity of Rubin's message was unmistakable:

March to your own drumbeat; call your own shots; do what you want to do for the reasons that are important to you—and don't let anybody lay guilt on you for doing it.

I told the editors about my interview with John Ehrlichman, the Watergate figure who had survived the soul-bending agony of personal and professional disgrace by deciding that he had to live his life by what he—and not society—thought was important. "I have a different idea of what is important now," he said. "What do I think is important now? I'll tell you: Will string beans climb cornstalks or not? That's what I'm trying to find out in my garden, and it's very important to me. What is very unimportant to me is what other people think about me."

Ehrlichman said there are two kinds of people:

—Those who "care enough about life to figure out what is important to them and who go and claim those things";

—And those who "never come to grips with the question and who let others supply the answers and tell them how to live and what is important."

Eventually, he said, some people in this second group "may realize that they are unhappy and that they have an opportunity to change. But probably only a small percentage will change. The others are miserable, and they never know why. Society continues to tell them how to live."

I told the editors that I had figured out what was important to me and that I had pursued those things—and that this was why I was satisfied and at peace with myself. The things that mattered, in order of importance, were:

—A marriage based on equality in which I didn't have to be everything to my wife; a marriage in which I could be both myself and a husband. Marilyn Funt, in her book that chronicled the lives of women who were married to famous men, wrote that behind every great man was a woman who was groping for her identity. That, I ventured, was no foundation for successful marriage. No, successful marriage was possible only when two "great" people came together—"great" in the sense that they loved themselves enough to love each other fully.

—A job that is fun and that directly touches the lives of thousands and thousands of people, many of whom respond with letters and telephone calls to say "thanks for what you've written."

—The freedom outside my job to do things that matter to me, if to nobody else. My first book, which was possible only when I no longer was an editor, had as its goal to explain to urban people what life is like on America's farms today, and it brought a kind of satisfaction that I never, ever found in signing personnel evaluations or affirmative action reports.

I told the editors that shortly before I had entered the convention hall for this speech I had encountered an old friend, Lou Boccardi, vice-president and executive editor of The Associated Press. Lou had asked, "What are you going to tell them—that they all should quit?"

No, I said, as my speech wound down to its conclusion, I wasn't going to tell anybody to quit. What I was going to tell them was that if they were in pain, they should try to find the reasons for the pain and then do something about it. "That's the only way you'll ever be happy; that's the only way you'll ever be free."

I sat down, and the applause thundered off the walls. They understood, but, I wondered, how many of them would act on their pain?

.* * * * *

The telephone call early that morning at my desk at *The Philadelphia Inquirer* was so similar to many that have come over the years, calls in which the wife says:

—She and her husband have been married for almost twenty years.

—Now he is becoming distant from her, withdrawing into himself.

—He seems no longer to get a kick out of things that formerly were important to him.

—He frets about his job and what he perceives as a lack of success.

—He complains about his relationship with her and finds fault with her easily—over things that wouldn't have mattered so much ten or fifteen years before.

—He spends less time with the children.

—He is moody, often for no apparent reason; sometimes he sits out in the yard, all by himself, and seems to be crying.

—He denies anything is wrong—and asks only to be left alone.

The question that every wife who ever called me always is this, "Is my husband going through mid-life crisis?" And then the next question invariably is: "If he is, how will it end? What will happen?"

I told the woman that morning that nobody genuinely could answer those questions for anybody else.

But I did talk to her about what I had learned from my own mid-life crisis and from dozens and dozens of conversations and interviews. Here it was, I told her, a short course on crisis:

—I believe it strikes every man at some time in his life—anywhere from thirty-five to fifty. It varies in intensity and duration, depending, usually, on how well you're put together psychologically, how solid your marriage is, and how firm the foundation of your career is.

—The crisis begins when the gnawing doubts you've had for years—about yourself, your marriage, your career, your life—stop gnawing and start biting. Worries about which you were vaguely aware come sharply into focus and you can't wish them away.

—Simple answers that once sufficed no longer are good enough. Once upon a time you could satisfy yourself that you didn't get a promotion because the company made a mistake. Now you face the horrifying reality that maybe the company didn't make a mistake. Maybe you're as far as you're going. Professionally, maybe you're at the end of the road.

—It becomes impossible to deny or ignore the harsh reality that you're getting older: You tire more easily. Even though you exercise and take care of yourself, your body isn't as hard as it was twenty years ago when you played football. Pounds are easier to put on but harder to take off. Your children are taller than you are. Your parents die. Heart attacks cut down some of your college classmates. You ask, Am I next?

—You recount the impossible dreams of youth and wonder what made them impossible. Silently and grimly you ask: Am I less than I thought I was? Less of a man? Husband? Father? Lover? Professional success?

—You wonder if your wife is everything to you that she might have been or could have been. Just how solid is your marriage? Is it strong? Is it merely OK? Or is it terrible—and have you been kidding yourself all these years?

The mid-life crisis becomes full-blown when you examine reality without the rose-colored glasses of yesteryear, when you separate the possible from the impossible and try to relinquish your grip on that which you never had a chance to get. This is when the pain can get almost unbearable, when you can sit in the woods and hug your basset hound and cry and wonder if it's ever going to stop hurting.

Yes, it does stop hurting, eventually. And if you have a close friend or two with whom you can share your doubts and your pain, if you make peace with yourself somehow, if you're just plain lucky, you can come out of the crisis stronger, wiser, and better than you were before.

How do you make peace with yourself? I believe you do it by isolating what you want out of life and deciding if its price tag is fair and reasonable. If it is, then you need to go after this dream—because it's possible. It may involve tremendous upheaval in your life, or it may involve no structural change at all, merely accepting yourself the way you are.

Can marriage survive the mid-life crisis? Yes, certainly, it can, and many times it's stronger than before. But sometimes it doesn't survive—and this is a reality that panics so many wives, including some who telephone me and want to know: "Is my husband going through a mid-life crisis?"

Without a doubt it is a tough time for many wives, who are being told to keep their cool while their world seems to be on the brink of collapse. But it's even a tougher time for many men who face the fire-snorting dragon of reality for the first time and who, in the beginning, don't know what it is.

* * * * *

Over the years it seemed increasingly evident to me that mid-life crisis might be viewed not only as a fast freight to pain but also as a stepping-stone to growth. Is that really possible for many of us in mid-life? I took that question to psychiatrist John B. Reckless at his clinic in Durham, North Carolina, not far from Duke University, where he once was a professor. Yes, he said, the mid-life crisis could be a blessing in disguise if we learned from our agony.

The evolution of mid-life crisis, as described by Reckless, typically followed this scenario:

The husband, at the office, begins to wonder: Is it worth it? He has the feeling that something is terribly wrong, that life must have more to offer than this. He has a title on the door, a big income, and prestige. But he also has an empty feeling.

He's puzzled, and he doesn't know what to do about it—since the demands on him to produce more financially are at their peak. The children are ready for college, and the standard of living is more than comfortable. The man may go in a number of directions to try to resolve the mid-life crisis. Among them:

—He simply may get depressed—and this is not

bad if he recognizes it as a warning signal and seeks help.

—He may deny there is a crisis, become depressed, and get involved in an affair. Typically these affairs begin nonsexually. He and the woman have long discussions, expressions of emotional needs. They share and spend time together. Strong sexual feelings usually follow. They feel quite close to each other. If they are mature, they'll seek counseling because they will realize that they're getting out of their emotional depth—even though they are enjoying the affair tremendously.

But entirely apart from moral considerations they have a better reason to consider ending the affair: the man is finding something better than he has at home. And this puts him between a rock and a hard place. He doesn't want to break up his family, sacrifice the affluence he's built over twenty years, and deprive his children of a "normal" home life. These factors either can cause the man to end the affair—or they can combine to deepen his depression.

—He may try to resolve the crisis by abandoning his job. Therapists see more and more middle-aged men doing this these days. They blame the job for every bit of their torment and feel that if they change jobs, all will be peaceful again. The problem is that two years later the man may wake up one morning and realize that foolishly he's thrown away twenty years of effort, because the job wasn't the reason for his depression.

Is divorce an inevitable by-product of mid-life crisis? No, not if the man gains more self-awareness and makes appropriate changes in his life. This self-awareness is the point at which the price a man is paying for success is greater than he is prepared to pay. At this point—and it may be reached after a heart attack, a problem with the children, a divorce ultimatum from his wife—the husband may be able to ask himself: What is driving me to work like a dog? Do I need that next step up the business ladder? Why am I always willing to take on another civic responsibility?

Often it takes something traumatic to force us into this kind of self-awareness. What we need, unquestionably, in our society is some scheme that causes us to take stock of ourselves and our marriages before crisis or divorce makes it mandatory.

While the man is wallowing and struggling, the woman may be depressed, too, and often it's the result of her having suppressed her feelings for so many years. Usually the depression isn't severe enough to cause her to seek psychiatric help, but without a doubt she is blue and miserable.

However, women are realists—more so than men—and they usually sense when something is wrong. They may plead with the husband to seek help. Often the husband will refuse and say he sees no problem. Eight times out of ten it's the woman who initiates the call for help. Many men feel this challenges their masculinity and their integrity. A man will ask his wife: "I've put you in a $175,000 house and I'm working sixty hours a week to keep you there. What else do you want from me?"

Is nobody exempt from mid-life crisis? Must it necessarily strike every one of us?

Psychologist Samuel D. Osherson of the Harvard

Medical School spoke to these questions in an interview in which he introduced me to the novel *Dubin's Lives* and the character who wanted one hundred lives because one was not enough. The reality of having only one life, Osherson said, was at the bottom of much mid-life depression, regardless of how much we have achieved.

Osherson explained it this way: If you make one choice, you always eliminate other choices. If you live one life, you eliminate other possible lives. If you grow up with the fantasy that everything is open, that the moon is possible, then no matter what, you eventually realize that the other things are not going to happen by virtue of the fact that your one life is being used up. This is when the chilled hands of depression and mourning creep into all lives. But the good news is that crisis is not an "F"—not a failing grade. Rather, it's a normal, expectable part of what it means to be human. The great literature through the ages is filled with discussions of honorable, decent men in normal lives who experience sadness at the finality of life, who mourned that they had just one life and not another.

The two factors most readily identified with crisis are job and marriage, and this has caused many men to believe that they could reverse their unhappiness if they changed jobs and/or wives. Often such a change failed to soften the crisis because the pain was coming from within rather than from the outside.

If such high-level change isn't the answer, then what is? Again, we come back to introspection. How well is the man able to tolerate some of the pain—and how much has he grown as a person in his career and marriage? What has he learned from the pain? Has it deepened his understanding of himself, his family, his career, his world? If there is little understanding of the causes of unhappiness, then there's not much reason to believe that a career change or marital change would help. But if there is some understanding and if it is accompanied by attitude and belief changes, then there is more cause for optimism. The question Where is the pain coming from? may lead to career change or marital change, but neither is necessarily the answer.

Some men continue the same struggles over and over again. They still struggle to be better than their brothers, still wonder why their wives don't understand them. They are successful in their new careers, but they still struggle in other areas of their lives because they haven't learned from what they've gone through. They still feel that they are victims, that the world doesn't understand them, that careers are terrible. And they have absolutely no sense of their roles in their own life histories.

What was Osherson's prognosis for mid-life crisis?

"Most men muddle through and make an OK situation of their lives. It is not a terminal illness—although many men carry it on their backs" for the rest of their lives. Those who tend to do best are those who have "some ability to tolerate sadness without feeling overwhelmed and who intuitively know to turn to others for help—a close friend, wife, brother, or parent."

There's not much a wife can do to help, he said, and this is why the man's mid-life crisis can be so devastating to the wife. "She can't force him to change. But she can show him that he is loved, tell him that pain is all right, legitimate, and that she's there for him. If he wants to go through therapy, she'll be with him. She can let him know that she is on his side." Is there nothing more she can do? No, because trying to speed up the resolution of mid-life crisis is akin to telling a scab to hurry up and form so the wound can heal. It just doesn't work that way.

* * * * *

As I examined my confrontation with discrepancy in the stark reality of daylight, I knew that peace would come to me only if I made in my life changes that amounted to gross amputations—changes in my career and in my marriage. There was no way, I knew, that I could manufacture in the executive editor's office the kind of joy and satisfaction that I wanted and needed. I'd tried futilely in the only way I knew—by beginning to write a column that publicly I'd said was to benefit the newspaper but that privately I realized was to try to ignite a ray of hope in days made dreary by reports, budgets, and testimony at unemployment compensation hearings.

There also was no way, I knew, that I could revitalize a marriage that now was rolling downhill and gaining speed, like a runaway train. The marriage counselor, during one of our private meetings, had acknowledged that when he told me, "Sometimes the best solution is dissolution." Others had suggested that to me before, but when the marriage counselor said it, within the framework of his $40-an-hour fee, it took on new meaning.

What I had to do was clear. But how would I do it? How could I do it? What would happen to Jay and

Grant, who, although they surely must know that something is chewing on Daddy's insides, couldn't possibly harbor the notion that Daddy might leave? After all, daddies are forever.

Chapter 7

The View
from the Lawyer's Office

I sat in the Charlotte lawyer's waiting room, fidgeted with my briefcase, and wondered why I hadn't taken more care when I dressed that morning. Yes, the gray slacks and the navy blazer were fine, but the white shirt with red stripes and the navy tie with white stripes clashed for supremacy. Unfortunately, neither won. Both lost and there I was, feeling like a loser, too. It's been written in every book since the dawn of time that on important days you should dress in clothes that give you confidence and help you to feel good about yourself. This was, in many ways, the most important day of my life because it was the first step toward closing one door and opening another—ending a long-standing marriage and beginning life again as a single person. Was I up to it? The shirt and necktie eloquently argued that I wasn't, and I was inclined to agree with them.

Could anybody ever be ready for this? No, don't think like that, I told myself. I had to be positive about it. I had made up my mind, finally, and I was going through with it. It wasn't like so long ago in Louisville when, late at night, I had climbed silently out of bed and walked down the hall to the room in which Jay and Grant slept in their stacked bunk beds, curled like tiny balls beneath their homemade bed-spreads of green and blue.

I had leaned against the beds, my head level with the upper bunk that held Jay, who was seven, and I had reached out and softly rubbed his back. Then I knelt beside Grant, who was six, in the lower bunk and stared at his peaceful face and unruly blond hair. "I can't ever leave you guys . . . no matter what," I had whispered. "I love you too much." And then I had sobbed, not because of the moment's tenderness but because I was trapped. I knew it and I accepted it. A responsible father doesn't leave his children—no matter what. Wasn't that the message that Pop and Mom had transmitted to me in so many ways—without ever discussing it directly? Wasn't that what they meant when they talked about people who lacked commitment and strength and who didn't have what it took to make a go of the biggest undertaking of their lives—marriage? "They can do what they want with their lives," Pop had said once, "but how can they ruin their children's lives? Don't they know that children need parents? It's just selfishness. That's what it is—selfishness—doing what feels good today and not caring or even thinking about tomorrow."

The words had burned into my memory. "Good" people don't get divorced. "Good" people don't leave their children. "Good" people work out their prob-lems. "Good" people deny themselves, if they have to, to keep the family together. "Good" people take themselves from life's center stage and, if it comes to it, they put their children's welfare ahead of their own.

It logically followed that if I wanted to qualify as "good," I had to keep the marriage together even though emotionally it long ago had begun to turn brown from lack of nourishment. For years I accepted the "responsibility" of being trapped. Jay and Grant now were into high school, and college loomed beyond with eight years of tuition that would keep my nose to the grindstone. On days when I felt good, I told myself that I could make it, that I didn't need the emotional and physical intimacy of an ideal marriage, that I could settle for less and maybe someday, when the kids were older and on their own, I could escape—if I had reached the absolute end of the line. On the days when I felt bad, I told myself that I already had reached the absolute end of the line. But the problem was that I couldn't escape. "Good" people don't escape; "good" people take life as it comes, swallow it, and smile.

But my boat had been rocked shortly before my fortieth birthday when I had interviewed psychiatrist Charles Starling on why age forty was such a milestone along life's passage. Forty was a time when we had to be honest, said Starling, who was a longtime friend and frequent golfing partner. Only I could determine honestly what needed to be done to put my life in order. I didn't have to be trapped unless I was willing to be trapped, he said. It was my decision . . . and I needed to make it—whatever it was—rather than drift along in the fog and complain about being unhappy. If I *decided* to stay in the marriage, then I ought to work with all my might to revitalize it. But if I *decided* to end it, then I ought to end it, stop grumbling, and get out. I had only one life to live, and

I owed it to myself to make it the best possible life.

"What about the kids?" I had asked.

"What about yourself?" Starling had answered. "They have their lives, and you have yours. You have to look out for yourself. You can't help them by hurting yourself."

He had looked solemnly at me and then asked with the bluntness that is acceptable only from a friend: "You want to leave, don't you?"

"Yes."

"Can't you fix the marriage? Can't you work out the problems or at least learn to live comfortably with them?"

"Charlie, I don't even *want* to fix the marriage. I don't even care enough about it to *want* to do anything about it."

"Then you ought to leave. If you feel like that, you'd do everybody a favor by leaving, especially yourself."

"But what about Jay and Grant?" I repeated.

"What about yourself?" he repeated. "You're trying to find excuses to stay, even while you're telling me that you've given up hope and don't even want to try to fix the marriage. That's crazy."

"Charlie, I'm scared."

"That's not crazy."

In the crunch of indecision, I did what I often advise others to do: I sought out friends who had grappled, with varying degrees of success and failure, with the same problem that now seemed to suffocate my very existence. What had they learned from what they had done or not done? If they had it all to do over again, would they?

* * * * *

Ron was in his forties, a banker I had known for years—before his divorce, when he invariably seemed subdued and beaten down, and after his divorce, when he seemed brighter and more outgoing but when he also appeared at times to have a heavy heart.

I asked how it had been for him—breaking up a marriage and leaving his two children.

"It was something I had to do," he said. "It was crazy for us to go on the way we were. We'd fight, and then I'd pack my suitcase and go to a motel for a few days. It got to where I didn't even unpack. I just left some essentials in the suitcase—and then I could leave in a hurry, when things got too unpleasant."

Had he ever been sorry? I asked.

"No, not sorry about the divorce. But I gave away too much. That was a mistake. I should have listened to my lawyer, but I didn't. I wanted out so much that I paid more than I had to. She wanted the house, and I gave her the house. Can you believe that? About forty thousand dollars' worth of equity, and I just handed it to her—and I got nothing out of it."

I asked if he and his wife had tried to resolve their problems.

"There wasn't anything to resolve. I reached the point where I didn't love her anymore. I didn't even like her. It was like I didn't want to be around her, and I looked for excuses to find things to complain about. When it's that far gone, you don't have a choice. You've got to get out—for her and the kids as well as for you."

How had the children reacted to his leaving? One

112

daughter was in high school, the other in grade school.

"They knew we were in trouble, but still I think they were surprised." The younger girl had cried, sobbed hysterically, and asked her father, "Will I ever see you again, Daddy?" The older girl had shrugged and wanted to know what kind of relationship the two of them would now have.

What had he said to his daughters?

He had tried to reassure the younger girl that his love for her was unchanged and that, yes, surely, they would spend time together, go to movies, to parks, to school events just as they always had. "I'm still your father . . . and I always will be." He had told the older girl that he thought their relationship would be better than ever. "I'll be happier—away from your mother—and that will make our time together happier. You'll see. Just give it a chance."

What had happened?

The girls had been drawn into a tug-of-war by their mother, he said, and they had been painted a picture that looked like this: "Your father has left me and he's left you, too. How can you be friends with him? A man like that doesn't deserve your friendship—and certainly not your loyalty." In the months that followed, the girls had backed off from their father, and Ron's response had been to give them ample space. "Look," he said to me, his voice rising, "they have their whole lives ahead of them, and they'll have to decide, sooner or later, how they want to feel about me and their mother. I can't lean on them to make up their minds now. They're hurt. Hell, we're all hurt, but kids are resilient. You can bend them out of shape and they'll snap right back—a lot quicker than adults. They will be all right. They will be all right."

How about you, Ron, will you be all right?

"It hurts. It hurts when your kids walk away. I wanted to grab them and shout: 'I'm your father, and you have to love me!' But they don't *have* to do anything . . . except, eventually, make up their own minds on what they want to do about me. I left because I had to—because it was too painful not to leave. I left to save myself . . . and the kids are going to have to save themselves. I couldn't live my life for them—as a father. I have to live it for myself—as a person. In doing that I think that ultimately I'll be a better father."

"Do you think they'll give you a chance?"

"I don't know. Someday, I guess. But I had my reasons for leaving. When you're dying, you have to look out for yourself."

"Do you feel as if you've saved yourself?"

Ron looked especially sad. "I don't know. I really don't know."

I told him about the decision that I would have to make about my own marriage. What did he think?

"If you leave, be prepared to hurt. No matter how bad you think it's going to be, it will be worse. No matter how much you think it will hurt, it will hurt more. No matter how ready you think you are, you'll find that you're not ready enough. Nobody ever is . . . I don't think it's even possible to be ready."

What makes it hurt so much?

"It's a failure. Anyway you cut it, it's a failure. The marriage didn't work . . . and now here I am as a father without any children. I really don't have any children . . . and that's what makes it hurt. I don't think it's possible to fail in marriage and not fail, to some extent, as a parent, too."

Ron wished me good luck and I left, not totally satisfied that he was the right person with whom to begin my quest. He hadn't told me what I wanted to hear. But then maybe nobody would. Maybe what I wanted to hear was a fairy tale that assured me that everybody would live happily ever after.

* * * * *

Bob was forty-seven, a businessman I had met on the golf course, a classic man in the gray-flannel suit who hid his emotions and showed no more elation when he holed a 20-foot putt than dismay when he skipped a shot into the lake. He was a hard guy to get to know, below the surface, but as I shared myself with him, he slowly began to crack the door on his soul. Bob was terribly unhappy and critical of himself and he was living his life by prefacing everything that happened with the question: What if?

For Bob, the What if? question amounted to this: What if he had left his wife and three children and seized what appeared to be his lifeline to happiness— a woman twelve years younger who was divorced and had no children because she wanted no children. They had met at a business party—she worked for a client—and from the very beginning, they had hit it off well. She was fun-loving, slender, astute in a deceptive kind of way, a woman who sometimes confused Bob with the blatant assumptions that she eventually voiced.

"Bob, someday you're going to marry me. You know that, don't you?"

"No, I don't know that. I already have a wife."

"Well, I'll wait."

As the months blended into years, Bob knew that Susan had been right: someday he was going to marry her because life would be better with her. She understood him . . . and she accepted the way he was. There were no demands, and what Bob wanted, Bob could have—if it felt right. If Susan had read the Carl Jung book on personality types, she undoubtedly would have discovered that she was a feeler—somebody who flew not by her mind but by her stomach. And that appealed to Bob. Nothing had to make sense—if it felt right.

With Susan everything felt right. At home very little felt right—except the children. They were the joys of his life, next to Susan—pleasant, well-adjusted kids who seemed to rise above the turmoil that swirled around them as Bob and his wife clashed more often.

The older of the two boys, a high school junior who played halfback and carded an eight handicap in golf, seemed to have with Bob the kind of relationship that every father dreamed of having with every son.

"Dad, I'd rather be here on the golf course with you than with anybody I know."

"Gee, Jerry, that's a nice thing for you to say. Why?"

"Because you have the membership."

And then they'd laugh. Sometimes it worked the other way.

"Jerry, you hit that drive like a gorilla."

"Yeah, Dad, I really got into that one, didn't I?"

"But the problem is that you hit your last putt like a gorilla, too."

Sometimes, they talked and nobody laughed.

"Dad, things are tough between you and Mom, aren't they?"

"We're having our problems. I don't know what's going to happen. How do you feel about that—about your parents having problems?"

"Everybody's parents are having problems. But I'm luckier than most kids. Underneath it all, I know you and Mom really love each other and us, too. I know you'll work out whatever it is that's bothering you."

"What if we don't, Jerry?"

"You wouldn't ever leave, would you, Dad? I couldn't stand it if you left. I don't know what I'd do."

"Jerry, I love you."

"I love you, too, Dad."

And they had embraced on the fairway, and nobody had stopped to gape. It was as if everybody knew that the moment was special . . . and not to be interrupted.

After that, things had begun to feel less right with Susan, and she quickly had sensed it.

"Bob, what's the matter?"

"It's Jerry . . . He and I were talking and . . ."

Susan listened, and she displayed no surprise. "Bob, we both knew that this wasn't going to be easy. I'm not putting any pressure on you to leave. I'll wait, Bob, until it feels right for you. I'll wait because I know that sometime it will feel right . . . because we're right—right for each other."

"Susan, I don't know if I—"

"It's OK, Bob, I understand."

But then the day had come when she had asked him to stop by her office after work—after seven thirty, when everybody had gone home. She had faced him, with tears running down her face, and had begun to read from a legal-size note pad that trembled in her hands.

"Don't read anything to me, Susan. Talk to me."

"Bob, I can't talk. I've thought all of this over very carefully, and I've written down what I have to say to you. Please . . . let me read it."

Susan had written that she now realized that they couldn't ever be happy together—not because they lacked love, which they surely didn't, but because of how Bob felt about his children. It was a beautiful relationship—too beautiful and too rare to shatter by divorce. She loved him too much to see him deaden himself on the inside by cutting himself off from his children.

"Susan, wait. I love you so much."

"You're a father, Bob. I can't destroy that without destroying you. I won't do it."

They had kissed and they had parted. Bob's reaction had been both crushing emptiness at what he had lost and a sense of elation at what he had not lost. He would work hard to rekindle the spark in his marriage, and the family would stay together and everything would be good again . . . as it once had been. In the months that followed he had tried, but he had come up short.

"Dad, what's the matter? You don't look happy anymore."

"Jerry, I don't know what you mean."

And from that day Bob had stonewalled it.

Through good times and bad, he was unchanged—at least on the outside. What was it like on the inside?

"I'm dead. I died a long time ago—after Susan left and after I found that I couldn't fix things in the marriage. I don't feel anything anymore because I won't let myself feel anything. If I did, I couldn't bear it because I hate myself so much. I sacrificed my life for my kids, and it was a mistake. Don't you do that. Don't you do what I did. If you have a chance for happiness, grab it . . . and don't worry about anything else."

It was rare that a day passed, even now, Bob said, when he didn't think about Susan and wonder what life could have been like if they had married. What if . . . what if . . . what if . . . It was a horrible way to live, Bob said, and he wanted to find a way out, but he didn't know how.

He, too, wished me good luck and I left, sad and more than a little confused. How could Bob let his love for his children become a wedge between himself and happiness? After all, wouldn't the children eventually understand that he had left not them but their mother? Couldn't he have it both ways?

But then I thought about Jay and Grant, and suddenly I wasn't so confused. It probably wasn't possible for anybody to have it both ways.

＊＊＊＊

Marlon was forty-one, a sales representative who always dressed as if he had vaulted right off the pages of a fashion magazine. He looked like a ladies' man, and women often responded to him that way, but Marlon was a straight shooter, and with Betty, his second wife, he was the kind of husband that all of us like to think we're capable of being—affectionate, kind, responsible, and faithful.

His first marriage had been a disaster, and while he didn't seem to enjoy discussing it, he would if approached by somebody whose questions seemed to have a purpose.

His two children were preschoolers when he had decided that the marriage was impossible and that the only way for him to survive was to get out . . . with the children. He shopped for the kind of lawyer who could get him what he wanted—a reasonable financial settlement and custody of the children. If he could have only one of the two, he wanted the children. He always could get more money, but the children carried his blood in their veins and never again could there be two children like them. He loved them; he wanted them; he would fight for them. If he had to, he would destroy their mother to get them. Without too much effort, he had found a lawyer who was a destroyer and he had won . . . everything.

How did he feel about what he had done?

"I like to think of myself as a nice person," he had begun, "but being nice has nothing to do with this. Being fair has nothing to do with it. Being human has nothing to do with it. You have to fight to win, to kill—like she's trying to take away from you something that's yours. Sure, the kids belonged to her, too, but they're better off with me. Even she would admit that. She never was much of a mother to them anyway—because they were too much trouble. They never were too much trouble to me, and in court they were able to establish that."

Marlon had been what the psychologists call "the

nurturing parent." and the judge probably would have broken tradition and given him primary custody of the children anyway—even if the lawyer hadn't brought out his big guns and leveled the woman. Yes, there were the witnesses who testified that, when she drank too much, she complained about how the children had ruined her life. Yes, there were the witnesses who said that, when she and Marlon argued, she sometimes left the house for a week without telling him where she was going. Yes, there were the witnesses who said that they had seen her coming out of apartments late at night, even a motel clerk was prepared to testify that . . .

She had thrown in the white flag of surrender and fled from the courtroom a beaten, broken woman. Marlon had not rejoiced, but he had told friends, "When it's kill or be killed, I want to be the one who's left standing."

Did he ever feel remorse about what he had done?

"I don't like to hurt people . . . if that's what you mean. But I also don't like to hurt myself. I knew what I had to do, and I found somebody who knew how to do it."

How about the children? How are they doing?

They were happy, Marlon said, and Betty was the kind of mother they needed. They never asked about their own mother, less because they had no curiosity, Marlon thought, than because they didn't want to anger him.

What had he learned from the ordeal?

"Fight for what you want. Fight any way you have to fight to win. Even if you don't like it—and nobody really likes it—do it. Otherwise, you'll lose . . . not just with the judge but with the rest of your life."

"That sounds harsh," I said.

"Life is harsh," he said.

Marlon, like the others, wished me good luck, and I left, uncomfortable with the notion that divorce was war and that children were the booty around which the most fierce fighting raged. Surely, it didn't have to be that way, did it? Did there have to be a winner and a loser? Couldn't everybody win—in some sense, however symbolic? Or—and the thought chilled me—might everybody become a loser?

* * * * *

The lawyer's receptionist jarred me back to the present. It was time for me to go in, she said.

I looked at the blue-and-white tie against the red-and-white shirt, winced, and walked through the open door. Never in my whole life had I felt more like a loser.

The lawyer was glad to see me, he said. After all, it's not every day that a newspaper editor comes calling. His warm hand grasped mine, and he invited me to sit down. "I hope," he smiled, "this isn't another false start—unless that's what you want."

I knew he would mention the "false start," because it was something that had to be cleared up. Two years before, I had gone to see him and and told him that I wanted to end my marriage.

"Are you sure?" he had asked. "That's a big step."

I was as sure as I could be, I had told him. The marriage hadn't worked for a long time, and I wanted out. I had made up my mind. Well, OK, he had said. He would write her a letter that announced my intention. That sounded silly . . . considering that we lived in the same house and had a chance to talk to each other daily. But in the legal profession some things did sound silly to people outside the legal profession. He would write the letter . . . and that would be the first step in what ultimately would be the divorce proceeding.

But the first step had been the only step. I had come home a few afternoons later, and she was there, the letter in her hand, and she was destroyed, devastated beyond my ability to comprehend.

The little voice of my conscience had not whispered; it had bellowed: "How can you do this to her? What's wrong with you? Wouldn't your parents be proud of you now—if they could witness this disgrace?" I had folded my hand and retreated. Probably, I wasn't ready for a divorce, friends told me, or else the little voice wouldn't have descended upon me with such impact. No, maybe I should bow my neck and try harder. Maybe there was hope, still, that the marriage could be saved.

If there was hope, I couldn't find any, and now two years later I was back in the same office and sitting in the same chair.

"I made a mistake. I backed off when I should have pushed. I'm ready to push now. What do we do?"

There would be no letter this time, he said. The best way would be for me to announce my intentions myself—after the fact. And the fact was that I was leaving. I should obtain the belongings that I needed from the house and *then* make the announcement.

Did I feel that I could do that?

"I feel that I can do whatever it takes. I know it won't be pleasant, but my whole life's not very pleasant now. I want to get on with living, and I have to take the first step sometime."

What would it be like, I asked him, not when I leave but in the months after that? What could I expect to happen? And what about Jay and Grant: Was there a pattern in how children tended to react when their father left home?

I should prepare myself to be hated, he said, only by my wife, he hoped, but possibly by the children too. I had to be ready for it—because it often came. In no other branch of the law does hatred run so deeply and last so long. It is this craziness by husbands and wives that ferments so many of the problems that shroud the children of divorce, he said, "and not the other way around, as a lot of people think. It's a rippling effect from adult behavior."

The hatred that daily walks into his office is beyond belief to anybody who isn't exposed to it regularly, he said. "I know of nothing in which people act with more violence than in domestic cases. Only in homicide is the hurt any greater. In homicide there ultimately is the recognition that the person is dead and that it's time to move on to something else. But the hurt remains in divorce—sometimes forever— because the other person is still alive."

The woman who is left by the husband often is devastated beyond description, he said, but there seems to be a direct relationship between where she has invested the bulk of her identification and how well she bounces back to resume her life. The woman whose primary self-image is as a wife flounders terribly when she no longer is a wife. If she's not a wife, she asks, what is she? She doesn't know—

because for years her whole self-concept has been attached to the man she married. Recovery from the trauma of his leaving often takes years—and sometimes recovery never really is complete, in the sense that the woman forever feels that she is less than she once was.

On the other hand, the woman who has been invested heavily outside of being a wife and mother—in her career or perhaps in hobbies or volunteer work—tends to regain her zest for life more quickly. She, too, has been wounded, but she has lost her husband, not her personal identity, and she is able to analyze her situation and plan her future without the paralysis of emotional numbness that lingers and lingers.

As the lawyer talked, I settled back in my chair, glad that he had seized upon my questions and run with them. Without doubt, he said, if divorcing parents would screen out their hatred of each other and not allow it to contaminate everything and everybody, the effect of divorce on children would be minimal. "Children normally are able to bend and relate in a new environment—whatever it is. They're not preoccupied with security. But kids are drawn into the upheaval of divorce by parents who insist that they take sides . . . and then they end up with guilt feelings that somehow they've caused the divorce. I've seen some nasty situations in which adults used the kids to fight their battles."

Never in his professional life, he said, had he ever had a case in which a man and woman entered his office, "announced their mutual nonlove and asked to resolve their differences by divorce. If this ever happened, there would be no substantial effect on the children. But what I see is one party that wants to leave and another party that is hanging on—not so much from love as from security—and this is the party that tends to bring the kids into the conflict."

Do the ages of the children figure in their adjustment to divorce? Surely older children handle it better than younger children, don't they?

He had to tell me, in honesty, what I didn't want to hear. His experience is that younger children are less adversely affected by divorce than older children. "You take a fifteen-year-old child who's given the choice of living with mom or dad, and the guilt that comes from making the choice can be tremendous. But a four-year-old kid who's living with his mother will miss daddy for two days and then he'll be back to playing in the sandbox."

The hatred that often is generated by the spouse who is left sometimes is so thick that it literally can be seen and felt, he said. "But I'll tell you something: In every case the hatred always works out badly for the hater. Eventually the hater falls victim to his or her own hate" through psychological or physical damage that results.

The hatred sometimes seems to stem from the notion that the person who has left has "failed in some way—especially if the other spouse now is with another person. The feeling is: 'I let him slip away from me; oh, how stupid I am.' " In this mind-set the haters are unable to think and behave rationally and often they want the lawyer to do for them that which is not possible—mend the marriage.

"You can sense what they want, and right away I will tell a woman, 'I can't make your husband love you.' And she'll say, 'Then you can't help me.' And I can't—if that's what she wants. She wants to fight to win back what is gone, and it can't be done.

"So she fights about who gets the frying pan—not because it's important but because it's a way of getting back. Winning becomes so big. Who gets the TV set is important even if you have a dozen TVs. If he wants it, he's not going to get it. It becomes a matter of competitiveness."

Not infrequently this competitiveness builds into a hatred that prompts one spouse to bring the children into court and force them to become advocates against the other.

"I was in court when one woman brought in her two daughters to testify against their father. One wanted to get at her daddy, but the other didn't want to be there. Why was she put in a position of being there? Because it's what her mother wanted. The one girl who wanted to sock it to her daddy testified that her mother wasn't able to pay the bill at the country club or at Montaldo's. She said that her mother had to sell a rug to pay the bills. How on earth would the kid know that unless her mother had primed her? That's how kids can get hurt."

In his experience, he said, the home environment usually improved after one parent moved out and the battling ceased—if the hatred could be kept in check. If both parents remarry, things can get better rather quickly—because hatred pales when people are preoccupied with building new lives. The children may not like the stepfather as much as their own father, but they accept the reality and finality of it and go about their business.

Other than that, the lawyer said, he didn't have much to tell me about the aftermath of divorce. Were there any more questions?

"What about the money? What's reasonable to pay right now, voluntarily, before she even hires a lawyer?"

The lawyer said that I should encourage my wife to make out a budget of essentials, and then I should send her a check for that amount every month—if I could afford it. What if I couldn't afford it? Well, there's where the trouble really begins, because it's fact that family can't live apart as cheaply as it can live together. Often there's not enough money to go around when the husband moves out, and this reality, when it comes to everybody, can snuff out any hopes for civilized divorce.

Even people who are not unreasonably angry with each other can go for the throat when money is the issue, the lawyer said. That's why he rarely saw a "friendly" divorce, because it seldom happened that there was enough money to go around.

One more question gnawed at me. I was reluctant to ask, but I did. If I paid her voluntarily what she said she needed, what was her incentive to get a lawyer and sign a financial agreement that would pave the way to divorce? I wanted a divorce—and as quickly as possible—because I needed to put the marriage behind me. I needed the finality that a divorce decree would bring. Was I risking a drawn-out divorce if I voluntarily paid the money? In trying to be fair would I be defeating myself?

Yes, very possibly, the lawyer said. Voluntary payments, if they were at all adequate, could be and often were stumbling blocks to settlement. If I wanted a divorce rapidly, he could tell me what to do. But, he said, "you won't like it and you probably won't do it. Most people don't . . . at least not right away."

"Is it illegal?"

No, it wasn't illegal, but the lawyer wasn't going to put himself in a position where he had to argue the morality of it. If I wanted a divorce as soon as the year's separation was up—the minimum time specified by North Carolina law—I had to be prepared at some point not to make any voluntary payments at all. Not any. It was what he called the smoke-'em-out strategy, and it seldom failed—at least, when it was used against women who didn't work outside the home and who were entirely dependent on their husbands for financial support.

But how was it possible, I asked, to smoke out the wife without smoking out the children, too?

It wasn't possible, the lawyer said, but that wasn't all bad—at least not from a strategy standpoint. When the kids got hungry, they tended to lean on the mother, and eventually this could provide added leverage for a settlement.

It wasn't pretty, but at least it usually provided momentum for a settlement that didn't leave the husband standing financially naked in front of the courthouse, the lawyer said.

"I don't believe I ever could do that," I said. "I couldn't put my kids through that. If we get stuck, we'll have to find another way."

That's how most husbands usually reacted, the lawyer said, and that was all right. But if things got bogged down, as they often did, then I might change my mind. Yes, he said, it was a dirty business. Nobody ever suggested otherwise.

I left his office after we had agreed on a strategy for separation, and I was committed to carrying it through to conclusion. I felt weak and shaky . . . and guilty. And I didn't need the blue-and-white necktie on the red-and-white shirt to make me feel like a loser.

Slowly I drove home—the long way. When I arrived, my wife met me at the door and asked me what kind of day I'd had.

Chapter 8

Separation: Silence, Loneliness, Craziness

The young woman behind the desk at the furniture rental company wore four-inch heels and jeans and a white sweater that looked as if they had been sprayed on her ample body. She smiled between smacks of her chewing gum and asked if she could help me.

"Well . . . yes," I fumbled. "I need to rent some furniture."

"That's why we're here. What do you have in mind?"

"I don't know. What do you have? I've never done this before . . . and you'll sort of have to help me."

What I knew about furniture I could write on the first two pages of a notebook, and the reality of that struck me between the eyes. Ours had been what sociologists call the "traditional" marriage. I had worked, brought home the money, assumed responsibility for the cars and the outside of the house and tended to the yard. She had been the classic mother and housewife, and the inside of the house belonged to her. I had no voice in the decisions that were made—not because she wouldn't listen but because I had little to say. I simply wasn't very interested. If she liked this carpet better than that carpet, she bought this carpet. If the living room chairs needed reupholstering, she decided if the new color would be green, blue, or cream.

When we built the dream house in the woods of the suburbs, she had gone to a junkyard and salvaged the scarred oak beams that would be just right for the ceiling of the family room. And then she had selected the wallpaper of red and gold to be pasted to the ceiling between the beams. It was an arrangement with which both of us seemed reasonably comfortable, although once she had expressed dismay when I had come home and announced that I had bought a station wagon that would be ready for delivery the next week. Like so many other things in the marriage, it was an arrangement that wasn't consciously arrived at. We had drifted into it, apparently on the low-level assumption that division of responsibility was easier and quicker than communicating and negotiating. The net result of more than twenty years of division of responsibility was that I knew as much about furniture and fixtures as she knew about cars and zoysia grass—next to nothing.

I would have to learn about a whole new life—not only furniture but also cooking, grocery shopping, cleaning, doing the laundry. It was my entry into the shadowy world of the unknown, and I felt insecure and inadequate.

"Yes, sir," the young woman said. "I'll be glad to help you. I have to help a lot of men . . . about your age. I'll bet you're getting a divorce, aren't you? Most of the men who come in here to rent furniture are getting divorced." She paused, mindful that she might be pushing the conversation beyond legitimacy, and asked, "How many rooms do you have?"

"Ah . . . two rooms . . . two rooms and a kitchen. Yes, that's it—three rooms." I had to stop and count because I'd rented the apartment sight unseen, and I had been inside it only once—on a day when the painters were there with their ladders and drop cloths. There had been two reasons why I had chosen the apartment: it was on the ground floor and opened directly onto the swimming pool, and I could afford it. The rent was $175 a month, and that was barely within the meager budget that I had allowed myself after I gave to my wife the portion of my paycheck that matched her budget. Actually, it was too much, because I'd left myself too little to live on, but I had fallen into the trap that snares so many men when they move out and end their marriage: I had tried to compensate for my guilt feelings by financial generosity that exceeded the bounds of common sense. After all, I had told myself, she and the kids needed the money to run the house. I could get by on what was left. But even now, at the very beginning, it was apparent that the squeeze would be tight.

Guilt always tended to be greatest right at the first, a lawyer once told me, and this was when mistakes were made that set precedent and sometimes put a man into a hole from which it was virtually impossible for him to emerge.

"I have one case now," the lawyer had said, "where a man is paying his wife far more than he can afford. He's doing it voluntarily, but he's doing it—establishing on the record his ability to pay that amount. Then one of these days he'll realize what's happening, and I'll have to go to court and try to convince a judge that the payments are too high and that in his ruling he should lower them. The judge will look at the record and say: 'Mmmm. He seems to have managed to keep up the payments before there was a court order. What's the trouble now?' And what am I going to say? The judge probably has twenty-five cases to hear before noon, so how am I going to make him understand that this case is special, that it's not a man trying to pay *less* than he can afford but a man who's trying to pay *what* he can afford?"

Guilt, the lawyer had said, was a predictable animal—predictable in the sense that it diminished as time passed. A man who was mired in guilt to the point of immobilization might be relatively guilt-free a year later, and his inclination to make high support payments likely would be blown away by the winds of financial reality. That's why, the lawyer had said, that when he represented a woman, he always tried to get an amount on the record as quickly as possible— while the man was wallowing in guilt. The more time passed, the more realistic the man would become about what he could afford and what was reasonable—and the more difficult it would be for the lawyer to get agreement on payments that would satisfy the woman.

The woman with the four-inch heels handed me a catalog with colored pictures in it and said that I probably could find something that appealed to me in just about any price range. The furniture could be rented separately—a sofa from this page, a stuffed chair from that page—or it could be rented in a package that included what was needed for from one room to a whole house.

"I believe I'll take a package," I said. "That would be quicker, wouldn't it?" I found what I needed by looking not at the pictures but at the rental prices. I needed a package that was rock bottom, and at this company rock bottom was forty-five dollars a month for two rooms and a kitchen. There it was, the so-called "penny-wise" package, which, the catalog said, "everybody agrees is economical, but some people even think is beautiful." I wasn't one of those who thought it was beautiful when the woman took me to the back of the store and showed it to me—a gold-colored sofa that felt hard as a board, a stuffed chair, an end table, a lamp, a plastic-top kitchen table, two plastic-covered chairs, a metal bed painted to look like wood, a nightstand, and another lamp.

The woman seemed to force an enthusiastic smile and she said: "But that's not all. You get your choice, at no extra cost, of a picture to hang on the wall or a plant."

"A plant?"

"Yes, sir, a plant . . . just like that one over there," she said, pointing to a red plastic flower that looked lonesome by itself in a green plastic pot.

"What about the picture?"

"Well, sir, you can pick from several. Do any of these appeal to you?" And she directed me to a row of plastic-framed pictures that were wedged between the sofa and a wall.

Without examining them, I told the woman: "I'll take a picture. Any picture. It doesn't matter."

I wrote a check and left after she promised delivery on time. It was a long, long way from the dream house in the suburbs—farther than I'd ever imagined.

How would I react to the Spartan life of a single person? Would the austerity and the loneliness be more than I had bargained for? No, I told myself, whatever loomed ahead had to be better than what lay behind, better than the residue of disappointment and disillusionment. I headed for a department store to buy a drape that would cover the sliding door that opened onto the swimming pool . . . and then I went to a junkyard.

Why to a junkyard? I wanted to buy some used bricks and some ancient timber and fashion them into shelves on which I would store the books that I thought precious enough to take with me on the day when I would move out of the house. Some of the books dated all the way back to college—*Law of the Press, Understanding Public Opinion, Editing the Small City Daily, Writing for the Small City Daily, Newspaper Reporting of Public Affairs*—books with covers scuffed by my handling through countless trips to classrooms and to the library, books that had little practical value to me now but that always would be part of me because they represented the learning years, the years that had reinforced my little boy's decision to go into newspapering.

I needed the books for another reason, too. A long time ago, in an interview, a psychologist who specialized in life after divorce had told me that a key to making it in the frightening world of being single again was to try to surround yourself with as much as possible from the happy parts of your previous life. I never had forgotten what he said, and before moving-out day I had decided which books I would have to have, books that had been housed in shelves that I had made and screwed into the wall in the suburbs, shelves that didn't look like much to anybody except me. I loved the shelves—because they represented the absolute limits of my carpentry skills, meager as they were. The day that the shelves went against the wall was a red-letter day for me—because it marked the first and only time I'd ever built anything with my own hands.

The shelves were in my study, which was in the front of the dream house on the ground floor and which looked directly out onto the sea of zoysia grass and transplanted trees. That was the room in which I had written some of my first stories that had been bought by magazines and in which I had rejoiced after I had run in from the mailbox, ripped open the envelopes, and found acceptance letters and, occasionally, even immediate payment. I couldn't take the shelves or the room with me, but I could take some of the books and perhaps through them the joys that they had witnessed in mute silence might again be tasted by me. That, of course, was what the psychologist had in mind, and I was taking it to heart—in a way that suggested that I really had no choice in the matter.

In addition to the books, the brick and wood shelves that I would construct would contain something else—a $105 stereo tuner that would give me if not hi-fidelity sound at least music that would shatter the silence of being alone. That mattered greatly to me—having something, anything, that would mask the reality that I was alone, that I no longer was part of a family, that Jay and Grant and their friends wouldn't be rushing through, that the crushing sounds of Grant's amplified guitar and the jauntiness of Jay's piano playing no longer would be part of my daily life.

Why was I so wary of being alone? Here I was, a man well into his forties who was professionally successful and who had done many of the things in life that he had wanted to do . . . and I was blanching at the notion of confronting the silence. Why? It was hard for me to believe, but the truth was that I'd never been alone, not really. I'd gone straight from home to college, where I always shared a room with another student. From college I had been drafted into the Army, where nobody ever was alone. I had gotten married and, when the Army turned me loose, she and I had moved directly into a tiny second-floor apartment, where the sounds from the family on the first floor kept us informed up to the minute on what they were having for dinner and on the extent of the parents' disapproval of their sons' late hours.

The silence was awesome, and not even the radio could break the grip that it held on me. I started to zip up my blue nylon windbreaker and flee from the apartment late on the afternoon of the third day, but I was halted by the telephone's ring. Who could be calling me? Only the office had my number, and it was too late—or too early, depending on how you looked at it—for anybody from the office to call.

Maybe it was Jay or Grant. My expectations soared. Perhaps they had called information for my number, and now they wanted to talk with me. Already they, too, had sensed the loss and they wanted to stop, back up, and get said the things that should have been said but weren't in the frantic moments of my departure from the house . . . or in the drugstore. Yes, surely, it was Jay or Grant. It *had* to be.

"Hello."

The voice that responded was deep and without a trace of humor. "Hello, my name is Gregory Laughlin, and I want to ask you a question: Have you made plans for what would happen if you suddenly left your loved ones? You would want to free them from the responsibilities of making decisions during that terrible period of mourning, wouldn't you? Let me tell you how—"

"Look, Mr. Laughlin, I—"

". . . to buy a cemetery plot right now with so little money that you won't believe it's possible. For just —"

"Mr. Laughlin . . . Mr. Laughlin, I—"

". . . pennies a day you can reserve a plot of your choice, a plot on a beautiful hillside with a view of the tranquillity of rolling farmland and the convenience —"

"Stop, Mr. Laughlin, I—"

". . . of perpetual care. Never will your loved ones have to be concerned about maintaining the property. I could tell you more—"

"Don't tell me any more, Mr. Laughlin. I don't want to—"

". . . but why not let us send you our free booklet, which contains the answers to all of your questions. At the sound of the tone, please leave your name and mailing address. Thank you for listening. This is a recording."

Good night, Irene. Mr. Laughlin wasn't even real. I

had been listening to a voice on tape, the victim of what the salespeople call random marketing. In other words, they just dialed until somebody answered. It was insulting, but it also was amusing—in a curious sort of way. Why hadn't I hung up immediately when I heard the sales pitch? Obviously, I wasn't in the market for a cemetery plot, so why had I held on to the telephone? The answer to that question came quickly and it added to the discomfort of being alone. I was so starved for somebody to talk to that I was willing to listen to anybody—absolutely anybody. I thought about the times that I'd screamed at Jay and Grant and demanded to know if they didn't think their father deserved some peace and quiet. I wished with all my heart that I had packaged some of their noise so that I now could open it and share it. I wouldn't holler at them to be quiet. No, honest, I really wouldn't.

Knock . . . knock . . .

Somebody was at the door, at *my* door. Well, at least it wouldn't be Mr. Laughlin. Random marketing hadn't progressed quite that far. At least I didn't think so.

I opened the door, tentatively, and there was a blond, curly-haired man who looked to be in his late thirties. He wore an ear-to-ear smile and a wool shirt of red-and-black plaid.

"Hi, I'm Gary, and I live right across the hall. You just moved in, didn't you? Well, no matter, you'll find that people here are friendly and easy to get to know. How'd you like to come over for a drink?"

"Well, ah, yes, thanks. I'd really like that. That's very nice of you."

"I've got to tell you, Mister . . . yes, it's Sifford, isn't it? Sifford, that's what they told me at the desk. I've got to tell you, Mister Sifford, that I really do want you to have a drink, but there's a price attached to it."

"A price?"

"Yes, you've got to help me move my new stereo into my apartment. The deliveryman left it outside and I can't handle it by myself. In fact, I can't even handle it with Charlie's help. Charlie's a friend of mine, too. He's at my place now, having a drink. Wouldn't you join us?"

Gary and Charlie were my introduction to what I quickly would come to consider the not-so-wonderful world of life as a separated man, a world that seldom included romantic cocktails in late afternoon with beautiful women but that often was stuffed full of drinking with other men whose presence seemed not to lift loneliness but to magnify it and whose passion for life seemed more projected than genuine. It was as if Gary and Charlie, and so many men like them, survived by fooling themselves into thinking that they were having good times.

Their definition of good times was to drink . . . and to talk about women they had known in the months since they had left their wives in search of fulfillment and happiness. It was both heartbreaking and terrifying—heartbreaking because they seemed in so many ways like homesick little boys and terrifying because I wondered if that was how others viewed me. No! I wanted to shout: I'm not like that; I'm different; I'm real! But I didn't shout it. I didn't even whisper it. Why? Because in the world of separated men, I perceived that nobody would want to hear that anybody was different. Misery loved company—even when misery was shoved underground and cloaked in the unbelievable disguise of good times.

Once in a while we sat—the three of us, Gary, Charlie, and I—and poured our bourbon into plain water glasses, nibbled on stale Kraft cheese and soggy Ritz crackers, and talked about what was real.

Gary hadn't *left* his wife; his wife had thrown him out after she had found him with another woman. She had been reasonably gracious about it, almost as if she had planned it for a long time—which she presumably had, since Gary's affairs were not unknown to her. She had told the children not that their father was a scoundrel, unworthy of their trust, but that he was a deeply troubled man who needed their love and support. They needed a father, she had said, and "by God, Gary, you're going to be a father to them! If you let them down now, you'll be sorry. I'll make you pay for it the rest of your life."

By the third drink, Gary was sobbing. "I'm lonesome. It was fun when I was married, running around with women. Maybe it was the excitement of doing it and not getting caught. But it's not any fun now. After a little while all the women start to look alike. They start to sound alike. And you know what's really awful? They're just as lonely and scared as the men. You know what they really want? They don't want to go to bed. Hell, they'll do it, but what they really want is for somebody to hold them, touch them, tell them that they're OK."

How had Gary figured that out?

"It's what I want . . . for myself. It's what every-

142

body wants—to be told that we're OK, that we're not always going to be looking in at the world from the outside."

Charlie was a fortyish man who dressed conservatively with a vest and a gold watch chain and who, without any encouragement greater than a few drinks, was eager to pull from his wallet pictures of his three children: Mark, who was fifteen; Debbie, twelve; and Jennifer, ten. He seldom saw them now because, after the separation, his wife had taken them home to her parents in Alabama, and even though the judge had ruled that they could spend a month each summer with him, he had no place for them to come. His one-bedroom apartment wasn't adequate, and so their visits together had been trips to places like Disney World, Six Flags Over Georgia, and once even to Disneyland in California. Charlie couldn't afford it, but he did it anyway—on his credit cards, which he then struggled to pay off for the rest of the year.

Why hadn't his marriage worked?

I'd asked Charlie that question before, and after one drink he had said that he didn't want to be married anymore. It had not been a hasty decision, but a decision that had been arrived at after much deliberation. It would be better for everybody to end it and stop the bickering. The marriage couldn't be fixed, and postponing the inevitable made no sense. It had been tougher than he had imagined—without the children—but he had made his bed and he was going to sleep in it. In time he would get his act together and decide what to do with his life.

When I asked Charlie that same question after he

had consumed three drinks and started on his fourth, he altered his answer substantially.

"I walked out because I thought I was in love with another woman, but after we moved in together it wasn't the same. All we did was argue, and then I realized what a mistake I'd made and I went back and asked Ginny—she's my wife—if I could come home. She wouldn't let me. She closed the door on me because she said that she never would be able to trust me again and she couldn't go through life that way. No, she said, she'd rather have us end the marriage— chop the whole tail off the dog, as she called it, rather than whittling it down a little at a time. It absolutely killed me. I still love her so much . . ."

By now Charlie was bawling and fumbling to get out a tattered letter from Mark, his fifteen-year-old son—a letter that Charlie obviously had carried in his vest for many weeks. In boyish scrawl Mark had written: "Daddy, I don't know why you and Mother couldn't get along, but I wish you'd try again. That's what Deb and Jenny want, too. We all want to be in a real home again and have fun like we used to. I miss you very much and I miss our good times. Please try, Daddy. Please."

Charlies' face was drawn in agony. "She won't let me come back. I've begged and done everything else I can think of, but she won't hear of it. We're not ever going to be together again, and it's all because of one stupid mistake I made. I'll pay for that stupidity for the rest of my life. It's not fair, dammit. It's not fair."

I finished the letter and handed it back to Charlie. He folded it lovingly and put it in his left vest pocket, next to the gold watch. "It's not fair . . . not fair," he repeated, and then he poured a fifth drink.

* * * * *

I hadn't seen Jay or Grant for more than a week—because I was hesitant to take the first step and risk rejection again. The sight of Grant's turning away from me in the drugstore seemed etched forever in my memory—and so did the hysteria-interrupted drive back to the apartment. No, I couldn't open myself to that level of pain again, but, yes, I so desperately wanted to see them. I dialed the telephone, and Jay answered. Would he and Grant like to have dinner with me Friday evening? We could go to Riccio's, our favorite Italian place, and have whatever we wanted.

"I think I'd like that," Jay said. What about Grant? "Well, he's not here now. I'll ask him, but I don't think he'll want to go. He's angry with you—angry and hurt."

What about you, Jay, I wanted to ask, are you angry and hurt, too? But I didn't ask—because I was afraid of the answer.

On Friday night Jay and I went out for dinner—without Grant, who had told Jay that he was too busy and "besides that, I don't want to go." We were at Riccio's, where the four of us often had dined, where the owner did the cooking, and where the lone waitress knew every regular customer not only by name but also by background.

She smiled her usual warm greeting, and I flinched when she opened with the question that I expected: "Where's your wife and other son? You're missing two tonight." I didn't answer. Instead, I slipped into the chair at the table to which she directed us, across from Jay. It was the same table at which I had sat late one afternoon many years before, waiting for the family to join me for dinner, sipping a beer and wondering what was keeping them. The waitress had come to the table and announced that I had a phone call. "I hope it's not bad news," she had said, but the tone of her voice implied that she was expecting bad news.

It was Verna, my wife, who said that Sherman, our basset hound, had been hit by a car, right in the neighborhood. No, he wasn't going to die, but he was severely injured—at least a broken shoulder and possibly internal damage, too. They were at the veterinarian's office now . . . and could I come?

I turned my thoughts back to Jay and asked him if he remembered the time when Sherman was hit by the car. Yes, he remembered, he said, and it was the most unsettling experience of his life . . . until that awful day when I had walked in and announced that I was leaving.

"It's really hard for me to accept this," he said. "I keep hoping that it's only temporary and that you'll come back."

"I wouldn't expect that," I told him. "I really wouldn't. That would not be a realistic hope."

Jay forced his head into the menu and said that he was going to order spaghetti and meat sauce with Roquefort dressing on the salad. It was what he always ordered when we came to Riccio's—and the memories washed back across my consciousness, back to the times when Jay and Grant were little, when they held my hands as we walked in from the parking lot, when, as I ordered a bottle of wine, they giggled in anticipation of the ritual that would follow: I would offer them sips from my glass and they would say, "Ugh . . . it tastes awful"—and then they would giggle some more, two little boys whose view of the world didn't extend much beyond the next block and whose faith in Daddy was without bounds.

"Jay, what are you thinking about?" I asked.

"I was thinking about how much fun we used to have when we came here, together as a family."

"We can still have fun—the three of us."

His face was solemn and his eyes were piercing as he stared at me. "Can we?" he asked. "I don't know how."

By the time the waitress came for our order, I had lost my appetite, but I ordered anyway—veal sautéed in butter and lemon juice. It was what I used to have at Riccio's so very long ago, but now it didn't taste the same. It shouldn't have surprised me, but it did.

Jay said that he needed to go directly home after dinner. He had a test on Monday, and he needed to study. I was glad that he had made possible a brief evening, because I sensed that his discomfort possibly was even greater than mine. We rode home in silence in the Opel GT that once had been our car of joy, and when he got out, he thanked me for dinner . . . politely and correctly, but not warmly.

The drive back to the apartment was not long. It just seemed that way.

* * * * *

Grocery shopping was for me the worst of the strange and unfamiliar domestic ordeals, not because I didn't know what to buy but because, to my amazement, I was uncomfortable in the supermarket aisles . . . with my cart and shopping list. It had been easy, I recalled with regret, to talk to the many separated men I had interviewed over the years and tell them that the adjustment couldn't be as difficult as they imagined it to be. It was a matter of breaking down the difficulty into its component parts and analyzing each, one at a time, and mastering it. That was the way problems were solved, I had said, and it could work that way in the adjustment to single life. All that was needed was a plan for attacking and defeating the problems.

Why was I so uneasy in the supermarkets? OK, I would try to follow my own advice. What was the core of the problem?

When I thought about it that way, it was not difficult to figure out. I shopped mostly after I came home from the office, usually late into the evening, after the massive crowds of the day had departed. The housewives had hurried home with their screaming, squirming children, and the aisles were nearly deserted. The few who shopped had no massive throngs of anonymity in which to hide. We were out there by ourselves, and, as we pushed our carts, we could look each other straight in the eyes.

"Why is he shopping all alone?" It was a question that I imagined they asked themselves each time they looked at me—because it was the question I asked myself each time I looked at them.

"Well, let's see now," I imagined they said as I tried to penetrate to the core of the mind. "Maybe his wife is out of town . . . No, I'll bet he's not married . . . Why on earth would somebody like that not be married? He looks like any ordinary businessman.

No, he's not married. Look at that—no wedding ring. And at his age. Good heavens, he must be forty-five. He's homosexual. That's it—of course. He's homosexual."

In the beginning, crazy as it seems, I had found myself keeping my left hand in my jacket pocket to conceal the reality that I wore no wedding ring and hadn't since the day I left home. Later—and even crazier—I had begun to put the wedding ring back on before I went to the supermarket, and I almost flaunted it in front of those whom I imagined were labeling me and taunting me with their judgmental indifference.

"See, see this!" I wanted to shout. "I am married—just like you!" But I didn't shout it—because at some level I didn't want to summon any scrutiny. In a bizarre way I had become paranoid in the supermarkets, convinced at times that others were concerned more about me than about their shopping.

"Good Lord, I'm going insane," I said, but the voice of reason, from somewhere deep in my mind, answered, "No, you're not—you're just going through a hard time."

Everybody, the voice said, was entitled to a little craziness in the crunch of life adjustment. Why didn't I just relax and examine what was going on and why? When I did, I threw the wedding ring down the trash chute. But just for good measure, I started shopping at midday so I could blend in with the housewives.

It was all so silly that I laughed about it when I described it to Gary and Charlie, who laughed, too. But I kept shopping at midday.

Chapter 9

Hard Work, Long Hours, Sweet Victory

At ten minutes past ten o'clock on a Tuesday night John Thomas Alford, who once was convicted of murder and sentenced to die, became a free man. He stood in a light rain outside the county jail, hugged his tearful-but-jubilant mother, and told her: "You're a super mom. I couldn't have made it without you."

Part of the crowd surrounding the mother and son surged forward and chanted hoarsely: "Free at last, free at last, thank God Almighty, he's free at last!"

At church Alford and his family attended a service of thanksgiving, and a minister prayed: "We know tonight we have seen salvation—before our very eyes." Another minister pronounced somberly: "God speaks from heaven, and we rejoice with tears running down our cheeks. The victory is God's, but he shared it with us. Thank God. Thank God."

* * * * *

At the office I worked longer and harder than ever before, not because I was more dedicated but because it filled the hours and kept me away from the paralyzing silence of the tiny apartment, the telephone that never rang, and the radio that seemed to play only sad songs.

I was surviving—each day seemed less bewildering than the day before—but it was far more difficult than anybody had warned me it would be. Jay and Grant were not to be heard from, and I didn't approach them, not because, as I liked to pretend, I didn't want to appear pushy but because I was afraid of what they might say or do or suggest with their eyes. At times I felt defiant: "OK, so you won't ever accept me or love me again. I'll get along without you." At other times I felt empty, weak, and vulnerable: "Please love me . . . please." But never once did I look back in doubt. Despite the pain, I knew that my decision to leave was proper—if I cared about my life.

The most compelling newspaper story on which I ever worked was throttling to climax, and I was glad, because I needed to be absorbed in something bigger than I was. I needed to be jolted with the harshness that my problems paled in comparison with the starkness of life and death.

This story, indeed, was bigger than I was—bigger than any one person except John Thomas Alford, a twenty-three-year-old black man who had been convicted of first-degree murder and sentenced to death in North Carolina's gas chamber along with an accomplice.

I had been introduced to the story a year before—after the conviction—when a physician I knew telephoned and told me that Alford's mother worked for him as a nurse in the hospital's dialysis unit. It was not possible, he said, that young Alford could have committed murder. He knew the mother well, and he knew the family's homelife. No, there had to be a mistake. Alford was no killer. In fact, Alford had no record of ever doing anything out of line. Would I do him, the physician, a favor? Would I talk to Alford's mother? Would I do whatever might be possible to straighten out this mess and see that justice was done?

I told the physician that I would look into it, but I said it without much enthusiasm. In years of writing and interviewing I never had met in a prison or in a courthouse anybody who ever admitted that he was guilty of anything. No, everybody had been framed . . . or else had become the innocent victim of a prosecutor's vengeance, a judge's prejudice, or a jury's incompetence.

At the hospital I talked with the mother, Mrs. Margaret Hunter, and, like the physician, I was touched by her gentleness and her concern for her son. We stood there, looking at each other, and she tried to smile, but she couldn't. "Please . . ." Nothing else came through her lips at that moment, but nothing else needed to be said. She was a mother, terrified that she might forever lose her boy. As a father who was terrified that he might forever lose his boys, not to the gas chamber but to fear, hate, and doubt, I instantly felt bonded to her.

She dried her tears and squared her face toward me. There was, she said, in existence somewhere a statement that the man convicted along with her son had given the police on the night they were arrested—a statement in which he said that he and another man had committed the robbery during which the murder had taken place. He had identified the other man, not as Alford but as Larry Waddell, who subsequently had been convicted of another murder and who already was serving a life term in prison.

I went to the courthouse basement and asked to see the Alford file. I leafed through the pages, not knowing what to expect or even exactly what I was looking for, but there it was—the statement—and, indeed, it plainly identified Larry Waddell as the killer: "I got the money out of the cash register . . . and Larry took the wallets and watches from the people. I came from around the counter and passed Larry and, as I got to the door, I heard a pop . . ."

Oh, Lord. I couldn't believe what I was reading. Had the law knowingly convicted the wrong man? Why? My subsequent interviews with the trial judge and the district attorney were even more baffling. Yes, they said, they knew all about the statement, but they didn't believe it. After all, there was such a thing as honor among criminals, and it wasn't uncommon for one who was caught to lie to try to set free a friend. By legal maneuvering the district attorney had blocked introduction of the statement into the trial record.

The Charlotte News streamed across the top of the front page the story I wrote about the buried statement. It was a story that flailed readers with the thunder of a springtime storm. The district congressman leaned on the governor to rectify "the mistake" with a pardon. The governor, through his press secretary, telephoned me to say that no pardon would be forthcoming. "What Alford needs is not a pardon—because that would forever leave a cloud over his head. What Alford needs is a new trial and an acquittal. That's the only way this matter ever will be completely resolved."

I mailed a copy of the story to the chief justice of the North Carolina Supreme Court, which heard the argument for a new trial for Alford. My telephone rang at twenty-five minutes before noon on a frantic, heavy news day, and it was our Raleigh correspondent, who shouted: "They gave him a new trial! A new trial!"

I began to pound out the story as my secretary placed two calls. The first was to Alford's mother.

"He's getting a new trial," I told her. "I'm on deadline. I need you to tell me something. How do you feel?"

"Oh, thank God . . ." Her voice trailed off in choking sobs.

The second call was to the district attorney.

"Pete, the Supreme Court has ordered a new trial for Alford."

He said nothing.

"Pete, are you there? The Supreme Court has ordered—"

"Yes, dammit, I hear you," he growled. "It's a rotten decision, a disgrace. We get this flack from people about turning criminals loose but when we nail one, the court wants to let him go. I'm mad, and I'm disappointed as hell."

The trial began on a Monday morning in the blaze of the publicity that I had ignited and that the other newspaper and the television people now had picked up. I was there when it began, seated in an empty jury box to cover my first trial, as a writer, in a decade. For seven relentless days the evidence was hammered into the record, and each day, as he entered the courtroom from his holding cell, Alford brushed past the jury box in which I sat and smiled faintly at me. I had talked to him only once—through the glass wall in the state prison's waiting room—but somehow I felt that I knew him and that he knew me. His attorney was James E. (Bill) Walker, the finest trial lawyer I ever had seen in action. Walker argued the case with brilliance, tenderly leading some witnesses but manhandling others with his booming voice: "Isn't it true that you've lied before? Isn't it true that you're lying at this very minute?"

During his 90-minute summation, Walker cried, not as a showman, I thought, but as somebody who believed fiercely in Alford's innocence. "I humbly ask you to right this wrong," he said. "I ask for justice ... and for mercy on a young man who already has been subjected to the horrors of death row for a crime that he never committed."

Walker turned toward me as he and Alford clinched emotionally, and I saw him whisper in Alford's ear. Alford nodded, his eyes glistening with tears, and rested his head for a flash of a second on Walker's shoulder. Then a deputy took him away, and the jury, after receiving the judge's instructions, began deliberating life and death at three thirty in the afternoon.

Alternately, I had studied my notes in the jury box and roamed the hallways, past the pay telephone into which for seven days I had dictated a lead and anywhere from five to eight adds as the courthouse clock tolled through deadline.

I asked Walker what he had whispered to Alford.

"I won't tell you. But you can ask John if you want to."

Alford's mother tugged at Walker's sleeve. "You did a wonderful job, Mr. Walker."

"Thanks. I hope you'll still think so after the jury comes back."

"Oh, it won't matter. No matter what, you did a wonderful job." She released his arm and turned away, trying to smile but crying instead.

The district attorney leaned against the glass-paneled door to the courtroom. He personally had prosecuted the case, and in his fiery summation he had commended the jurors to "send a message to all killers" by convicting Alford.

"What do you think, Pete?" I asked.

He was civil but not friendly. "I think I convicted the right man for the second time. I know I did."

At nine forty-five—more than six hours after they retired—the jurors signaled with two raps on the door that they had arrived at a verdict. They filed into the courtroom quietly, and most of them looked at their feet. But wait; what was that? Yes, a black woman on the jury quietly had flashed a tight smile toward Alford, who had seen it and turned toward me, his face inquisitive, as if to ask, Did you see it, too?

The judge, a son of former North Carolina Senator Sam J. Ervin, confronted the jury: "Ladies and gentlemen, listen to what I ask you and tell me no more than your answer to what I ask. Have you reached a verdict?"

"We have, your honor," said the jury foreman, an

Eastern Airlines employee in a white, open-neck shirt.

The moment of truth was at hand. The judge's strong, firm voice asked, "Is the verdict in the case of the state versus John Thomas Alford guilty or not guilty?"

The jury foreman paused ever so briefly, and in that instant I looked first at Alford and then at the district attorney. Alford had folded his hands on the table before him, and he was staring directly at the foreman. The district attorney, who had loomed like a giant during his prosecution, now looked frail as he sat behind his table and squinted down at his necktie.

"Not guilty."

The courtroom exploded, and the judge rapped his gavel for quiet, but the explosion continued. "Mr. Sheriff, Mr. Sheriff!" the judge cried. "Arrest anybody who contributes to this confusion. I want order! I will have order!"

The uproar nearly drowned out the judge. And there was Alford, crying, embracing Walker, shaking his hand. Then Alford was gone, whisked out of the courtroom and returned to jail, from where he would be set free. The judge thanked the jurors and dismissed them. I homed in on the black woman who had smiled at Alford.

"Miss, Miss . . . Was the jury in agreement all along?"

"No comment. I'll have nothing to say to anybody." Her face was grim. No doubt about it, I'd have to go without any comments from the jury. The jail was one short block away, and I ran, as fast as I could, down the street to where the television floodlights and camera crews had assembled and where Alford's friends waited, delirious with joy.

"John! John! John!" they shouted.

The door opened, and Alford emerged, immaculate in a gray suit and white shirt. His mother was beside him and he hugged her and cried.

"John! John! John!" they shouted even louder.

And then: "Free at last, free at last, thank God Almighty, he's free at last!"

It was the stuff of which very good movies are made. I was buffeted by the crowd and perhaps twenty-five feet from Alford when he looked up, recognized me, released his mother, and forced his way in my direction.

"Hi, John. I'm so happy for you."

He shook my hand, then he grabbed me around the neck, pulled me close, and said: "I want to thank you for what you've done for me. Thank you very much."

Justice, in my opinion, finally had been done—as much as possible, considering that he had been in prison for a year. I rejoiced for him . . . and with him.

I went with him and his family to the church service and then we drove to the mother's house, where Alford vaulted out of the car, pulled off his shoes and socks and ran his feet through the grass. "You have no idea how good this feels, how long it's been since I've had grass under my feet. In prison, you know, they don't have grass. They have concrete."

We gulped down fried chicken and root beer, and Alford talked between mouthfuls. No, he said, he didn't hold bad feelings against the witnesses who had testified against him or the district attorney who had prosecuted him. "They believed I was guilty," Alford said. "I'm sure they wouldn't have done it if they'd known I was innocent."

What, I asked, had Walker, his lawyer, whispered to him before the case went to jury?

"He told me he'd done the best he could and he hoped it was good enough. He's a great man, isn't he?"

It was after three o'clock in the morning when I toppled into bed at the apartment, fatigued physically but invigorated emotionally. I rolled over to go to sleep, and in my last conscious moments I saw in my mind's eye not Walker, not Alford, but Jay and Grant Sifford.

Chapter 10

A Night of Terror,
Days of Reflection

The dawn broke and revealed a cloudless sky that looked more black than blue on the morning that ushered in what would become the most terrifying night of my life. In the Carolinas people are fond of proclaiming that this kind of day is ordinary even in late January—a morning low of 28 degrees and a midafternoon high of 57 degrees, a day when you can play golf in a lightweight wool sweater and be perfectly comfortable except when the wind funnels through the pine trees and across the lake on the eighteenth hole. That's when you pull the nylon windbreaker from your bag and anticipate how good that strong black coffee will taste in the men's grill.

Maybe I would get in a few holes late in the day, I hoped as I scanned my pocket calender in an early morning ritual that had been with me for as long as I could remember. There were the usual newsroom meetings that began with the nine o'clock news conference and ended with the sometimes frantic, on-the-run briefing with the managing editor when we decided, about noontime, exactly how we would assemble the final edition.

At one thirty I had to be in the personnel office to

discuss this month's affirmative action report, and after that the general manager wanted to know if it would be possible to chip another five percent out of the year's budget. No, it wouldn't be possible, I would argue, unless he wanted to tell me not to fill the four new jobs we had built into the budget. It wouldn't take me long to say that, and I might be headed for the golf course by three thirty. That would be enough time for a rapid nine holes before darkness clamped down and the expressway became clogged with the bouncing headlights of people who were fleeing their offices in the city for their homes in the suburbs.

I would have a leisurely dinner of hamburger on a kaiser roll, green beans out of a can, and a salad with chopped mushrooms—that was about the limit of my creativity and know-how in the kitchen. Then I would be off for the radio station where I was the guest for tonight's talk show.

The radio talk show clicked past quickly with the usual blend of friendly questions—"How on earth do you ever find so many interesting things to write about?"—and hostile questions—"Do you really sell many more newspapers when you put those stories about sex and violence on the front page?"

By a few minutes after eleven I was out of the studio and on my way home . . . no, not really home, because the apartment didn't seem like home, and, frankly, I hoped that it never would. It had no warmth; it had no color; it had no sound. Some days I felt that it had no hope either, but then, I reminded myself, that wasn't the apartment's fault. The apartment merely was reflecting back at me what I was feeling but seldom saying aloud. After all, how could I tell even a close friend that I now knew that hope didn't always spring eternal, that on some days chocolate chip cookies had the taste of vanilla wafers? No, on those days I wouldn't talk about it; I would play golf, and a few whistling drives and a handful of bottom-of-the-hole putts would neutralize what sometimes approached despair and bring back the sunshine of hope and the taste of chocolate.

I boiled enough water for a cup of decaffeinated coffee, munched a bite from a week-old cookie, and prepared for bed. My gray-flannel suit, wrinkled from the long day's wear, was on the hanger now, and I was popping out my contact lenses.

At three minutes before midnight the telephone's jangle overrode the radio's volume. It was a weird time for a call, but I was listed in the telephone book. Maybe somebody wanted to discuss the radio show.

"Hello."

"I . . . thought you were good . . . on the program. Jay taped it, and maybe sometime, if you want, you can come over and listen to it."

It was unmistakably Verna's voice, but something was wrong. She was speaking haltingly, as if she were either terribly frightened or crying—or both.

"What's wrong? Is something wrong?"

"It's . . . Grant . . . and there's been an accident. I think you'd better come. Can you come . . . right now?"

There it was, I thought grimly—the midnight call that every father of a driving-age son must await with dreadful anticipation. And now it was happening to me. I didn't want to believe it.

"What kind of accident? Was he in the car?"

"Yes . . . It happened just up on top of the hill, on Tottenham Road, right at . . . the curve. Can you come . . . right now?"

"Is he hurt? How badly is he hurt?"

"I . . . don't know. Come now . . . please."

"Do you want me to pick you up?"

"No, Jay and I will already be there. Hurry. Please hurry."

The distance from my new apartment to my old castle in the suburbs was twelve miles. At this time of night I could make it in fifteen minutes. I jerked the gray-flannel suit onto my body and ran mindlessly toward the parking lot, leaping across a corner of the swimming pool and brushing past the wire fence beyond which my still-warm car waited for me. I jammed forward the headlight lever on the Opel GT with such force that the retractor that rotates the headlights into position went haywire. The left headlight came up and bore a bright beam straight ahead into the darkness, but the right headlight froze halfway up, and its ray pointed crazily toward the horizon.

"Oh, damn, not now!"

I spun the car out of the lot, spraying the loose stones atop the asphalt and speeding through the first red light that tried to stop me. My hands were slick on the steering wheel, and my mouth was dry and filled with the taste of gunmetal, which always is present when I am scared out of my wits.

Over and over I found myself crying: "Oh, God, please don't let him be dead when I get there. Oh, God, please don't . . . please don't let him be paralyzed." And then I was screaming: "No! No! No! This can't be real! It's not really happening!"

What would I find when I got there? Would he still be there? Would a doctor in the neighborhood be there? Would somebody be there to help? The accident had happened on that sharp, uphill curve on Tottenham Road, not more than four blocks from our home, but for heaven's sake, it's a residential neighborhood, and it's not a hard curve to handle at a reasonable speed. How could it have happened?

I skidded around the corner from the main road and into the Kingswood subdivision and oh, my God, there it was—the accident. The blue lights of two police cars and the red lights of an ambulance flashed and smeared color on the trees, the houses, and the people who stood back from the edge of the road, some of them clutching children by the hand.

My white Buick station wagon was off to the left, crumpled, as if the front end had been wrapped around a three-foot-thick tulip poplar tree that stood guard near the front bumper, from which hung bits of tree bark. I gasped when I looked at the windshield, which was punctured directly in front of the steering wheel. That could mean only one thing: Grant had not been buckled up, and his head had impacted into the windshield.

Grant had turned sixteen just eighty-one days before . . . and now there he was, lying face up on a blanket ten feet from the wreckage. On the ground he looked almost tiny, so much shorter than his six feet, four inches, so terribly vulnerable, so horribly disguised by the blood that flowed from his head and matted his blond mustache. It was not possible immediately for me even to recognize him as my son.

A physician who lived across the street was kneeling in his red plaid bathrobe beside Grant. He looked up at me, forced a nod of recognition, and said: "His neck's all right. He's not paralyzed. But his leg is broken and he's badly cut up. Badly." Then he bent down into Grant's face and said softly, "Grant, your father is here."

Grant's lips moved, but no sound came out. He moved his head slightly and spit blood onto the blanket.

"Grant, it's Daddy. Can you hear me?"

His voice was weak but his words were well formed and understandable. "I'm OK. I don't feel too bad." And then he mumbled something that wasn't understandable.

"I can't hear you, Grant. What did you say?"

"I'm sorry about the car. I'm really sorry."

"It's OK; it's OK; it's OK. Don't worry; please don't worry."

"I'm all right, I think. How's David?"

David Snepp was fourteen, the other boy in the car, Grant's next-door neighbor, the son of Superior Court Judge Frank Snepp, a longtime friend of mine. David and Grant, I would be told later, had been coming home after dinner with two friends when Grant missed the curve, knocked down a string of mailboxes, and skidded into the tree, causing, neighbors would say, a sound that resembled an explosion.

The ambulance crewmen seemed efficient and confident as they applied a temporary cast on Grant's right leg. Then they carried him on a stretcher to the ambulance, where, for the first time, I saw Verna.

"You want to ride with me to the hospital?" I asked.

"No, I'll go in the ambulance. It's awful, isn't it?"

"I don't think it's as bad as it could be. He seems alert. He's not paralyzed." It was all the optimism that I could muster through my stupor of fright.

Verna's eyes were red and brimming with tears, but her voice seemed uncommonly peaceful. "Will you find Jay and talk to him? He's so upset. The Brownings up the street are going to keep him at their house for the night. He's so upset."

Jay was across the street, all by himself, his camel-colored car coat unbuttoned, his hands jammed into the pockets. He stood there, as motionless as a statue, as I approached, and then he erupted in tears, folded his arms around my neck, and cried: "It's so terrible. So terrible." I had my arms around his shoulders, which heaved convulsively as he sobbed. "It's so terrible."

"Yes, it is, but he'll be all right. I'm sure that he'll be all right. Will you try to get some sleep?"

"I don't think I'll ever be able to sleep."

"Will you try?"

"Yes, I'll try."

Verna was in the front seat of the ambulance next to the driver. The other crewman was in the back with Grant. The siren broke the stillness, and the ambulance careened out of the subdivision, its red lights still flashing their message of urgency. David Snepp, who was complaining of stomach pains, got into the car with his father, who drove him to the same hospital. I sought out one of the two policemen who remained and told him, "Thank you for coming."

It was a crazy thing to say, but I felt crazy and I wasn't embarrassed. "Thank you for coming," I repeated.

The policeman seemed puzzled. "Yes, sir," he said, and then he walked away.

The emergency room at Charlotte Memorial Hospital was not an unfamiliar place for me. Just three months before, I had spent part of a weekend there, preparing a story on the people who work there, people who deal daily with life and death, reality and unreality, and who still manage to smile, most of the time, at shift's end. But, I thought as the sliding doors responded to my footsteps, arriving as a parent was starkly different from coming as a writer. Before, I merely was gathering information; now, I had an investment, a heavy investment.

A nurse who recognized me smiled and said: "Mr. Sifford, your wife is down the hall in the waiting room. Grant is in emergency room number 16. Please have a seat. The doctor will be with you as soon as he has something to tell you."

In the early morning hours of a weekend a hospital emergency room takes on the character of a battle-field as the wounded from fights and the injured from accidents are wheeled in for stitching, surgery, or reconstruction. Before, the drama had absorbed me; now, I hardly was conscious of the organized confusion and the intercom urgency of "Paging Dr. Hart; Dr. Hart, please." That, I knew from my earlier visit, was the hospital's code for announcing a coronary emergency, a code that would send the cardiac team racing to the intensive care unit. There was another code I had learned, too: "Paging Dr. Redd. Dr. Redd, please come to the fourth floor." That announced a fire without unduly alarming the patients. If the fire was minor—as it usually was—most of the patients never even knew about it.

Verna was restless in the waiting room, her hands fidgeting in her lap, her lips drawn, her face pale. She smiled and I smiled back, but not a word was spoken. Time seemed to hang in a vacuum. What time was it, anyway?

A resident physician ducked out of emergency room number 16 and confronted us. "I've looked at some of the X-rays. Your son's thigh is broken and his skull is fractured, but his chest looks fine. I don't see any evidence of injury there. That's all I can tell you at this time." With that he disappeared down the hall.

I walked to the coffee machine. It was one fifteen on Saturday morning, and the pace was quickening as stretchers were wheeled up and down halls and in and out of surgical rooms. At the nurses' station one nurse said to another, "If this doesn't slow down, we're going to have to start hanging them from the ceiling."

On another night in another circumstance I might have chuckled. Tonight I found nothing funny, and I had to restrain myself to keep from saying, "If it were your child . . ."

On the way back from the coffee machine I encountered a uniformed city policeman, who stood in the corridor, beside his wife, with his face pinched in torment. He said to me, "I'm really sorry about your boy."

I thanked him and asked him why he was at the

hospital. His two children, he said, had been walking near their home and had been forced to dive into a ditch to escape a driver who seemed to swerve in a deliberate attempt to hit them.

"They aren't really hurt," he said. "They're frightened. I'm frightened, too. And angry. Why would anybody want to do that—try to run over two kids who were walking along and minding their own business? And the driver never even stopped. Good God, he must be insane."

I told him I was sorry, and then I returned to the waiting room with two plastic cups of coffee. Verna and I no longer were alone. In the room, in a chair over in a corner, a man in his early twenties sat with his face buried in his hands. Suddenly he jerked to attention at the sound of a stretcher's being wheeled past the doorway, which revealed a young woman with her head extensively bandaged. In a flash the man was on his feet, following the stretcher.

Later he would sit with us and with misty eyes talk about the woman on the stretcher:

"That's my girl friend, She was driving tonight—with some other girls—and she had a wreck and she went out through the windshield. And they tell me her right ear is severed. Cut off. Oh, Lord, what I'd give to trade places with her. I wish it could be my ear that's missing . . ." His voice trailed off, and his head went deep into his trembling hands.

Outside in the hall a uniformed policeman with a mane of hair that hung below his collar appeared with a pencil and report form and confronted a nurse. He was looking for "the victim of an assault," he said, and he needed to ask more questions to complete his paperwork.

The nurse stared at him in disbelief. "The victim of an assault? You'll have to be more specific than that. We have thirty-seven people in here and more than half of them are victims of assault. We have one woman that somebody poured gasoline on and set afire. Is she the one you're looking for? If she is, you'll have to wait."

The policeman shrugged and left, without another word.

From the doorway I saw movement at Grant's room. A physician in a green surgical suit emerged—this shift's orthopedic man. He smiled politely. "You want to look at his X-rays? Come on."

Verna was beside me, her cold, moist hand gripping my wrist. We walked behind the physician through the swinging doors of emergency room number 16, and there was Grant, face up, his right leg suspended in traction, his head still as bloody as before. The sight jarred me because the man bending over him obviously was not a physician but another emergency patient. He was a black man with a bandaged right hand, a green T-shirt, and a green golf cap, and he was telling Grant: "Buddy, you're going to be all right. I know you are. Just keep it together, Buddy; you're going to be all right."

Later the man would say that he was walking home from work when three men leaped from the darkness, grabbed the package he was carrying, and slashed him with a knife, almost severing his thumb. "This whole thing is crazy," he would say. "I'm from Detroit, and everybody says Detroit is a tough town.

Well, I'll tell you, Buddy, Detroit's not as tough as this place. I've never seen nothin' like it. You can't walk home from work without somebody cutting on you."

On the table Grant stirred, ever so slightly.

"You doing all right, Grant?"

"It . . . hurts. It . . . really . . . hurts." His voice was markedly weaker than before. His eyes were partially opened, but I was certain that he was not seeing me.

The physician motioned toward the X-rays, which showed that Grant's right thigh bone was splintered, separated about halfway between hip and knee. The doctor said that he sees "quite a few" breaks like this. No, there would be no permanent damage, no limp "if we do what we're supposed to do." He smiled brightly. "And we usually do what we're supposed to do."

But it would be a long time—months—before Grant was up and walking again, the physician said. That meant that there would be no baseball this season. I wondered if there would ever be another baseball season for Grant. He pushed off that right leg when he threw off the mound—and would the leg ever again be strong enough? I thought about the last time I'd seen him in uniform, when he stalked off the field after being knocked out in the late innings of a Babe Ruth regional championship game. He had thrown hard, but the batters had hit him hard, and he hadn't been cheered by my later reminder: "Well, there's always next year." Now there might not be a next year—ever again. The thought almost was too grim to confront, and I felt guilty and a little silly. How could I think about baseball tonight?

But baseball had been such a big part of our lives, mine and Grant's, literally a glue that helped hold us together during the years when teenagers tend to propel themselves away from the parents in a hurry-up quest for independence. Grant had moved away, but baseball always had brought us back together.

There was the time, when he was a sophomore, when he had pitched and lost a five-hit game on Friday and then come in as a relief pitcher on Tuesday with the bases loaded and nobody out. On six pitches he struck out the first two batters he faced, and then he picked the runner off second base. Unbelievably, the inning was over, and nobody even had fouled a pitch off him. I asked him if he wanted me to drive him home after he showered, knowing full well that he would thank me politely but say that he would ride with friends. He surprised me. "Yeah, I wish you'd wait. I'd like to talk to you about the game. Wasn't it something?"

Now there he was on the table. Baseball seemed so long ago and far away. His mother gripped his bare upper right arm, closed her eyes and moved her lips in a silent prayer. I held Grant's left hand, which was cool and dry.

Somebody in a white jacket wanted to know if I had a preference for the plastic surgery that needed to be performed this very morning. "You want us to get somebody?"

"No, please call Dick Giblin, will you?"

Dr. Richard Giblin was a longtime friend, a tall, lean man with a quick wit and a ready smile. I had interviewed him twice in years past and he had made available to me his album of before-and-after photographs of some of his patients. It was an album he kept, he said, as a reminder of what it was possible to do in situations that sometimes seemed impossible.

He arrived a few minutes before 3 A.M., looking fresh, ready, and all business. There was a brief greeting and polite conversation that seemed forced. This was not the Giblin with whom I had shared cocktails; this Giblin was a different man, the working man. He examined the X-rays and told me that the outer layer of bone in Grant's forehead was fractured, that a chip of bone was missing, that this might result in Grant's having a depression in his forehead for a while. "But we'll worry about the cosmetic problems later," he said. "Right now we need to get his face stitched back together."

He left to put on his surgical suit, but Grant's surgery would have to wait. Only one operating room was immediately available, and David Snepp's physician wanted to use it for exploratory surgery. "His stomach is very hard," he told David's father. "I don't like the way it feels. I want to go in there and look around. I don't know what we'll find. I don't want to alarm you, but it could be something rather dangerous."

I inched close enough to them to hear the physician mention "colon" and then "colostomy." Judge Snepp's face was stern. "Do what you have to do."

Later David Snepp would be surgically treated for a torn intestine—suffered when the force of the accident thrust him forward against his tightly strapped seat belt. In a week he would be out of the hospital.

His doctor would say that "we're seeing more injuries like this, where internal damage is caused by the seat belt. I'm not saying that he'd have been better off without a seat belt. I'm saying that maybe he traded his injury for his life. Your son wasn't wearing his seat belt—and look at what happened to him."

Dick Giblin sewed on Grant's face until after five thirty on Saturday morning. When he finally emerged from the operating room, he lowered his green mask and without a word his appearance announced that he no longer was fresh and ready. He looked tired, and his face was thin and drained of color.

"He was a good patient. He was awake during all of it—we used a local anesthetic. He talked with me all through it."

"How many stitches?"

"I didn't count them."

"A hundred?"

"Oh, more than that. Maybe 150."

In the operating room Grant wore clean bandages. His right eyelid, split in the accident, was neatly stitched back together. There was no eye damage, Giblin said, "but if the cut had been a fraction of an inch longer . . ." I was glad he didn't finish the sentence. I didn't want to hear it.

I leaned close to Grant. "The doctor said that you were a good patient. How do you feel?"

His voice was strong, but his speech was slow. "I never thought anything could be that bad. It hurt like hell. I felt every stitch. It was like he was sticking in a fishhook and pulling it out."

"You're going to be OK, Grant. The doctors told me you'll be as good as new in three or four months. We're really lucky."

"How's David?"

"They operated on him for a perforated intestine."

"Oh, no . . ."

A tear washed down Grant's left cheek and disappeared into his mustache. I turned away and stared at the floor.

Somebody else in a white coat told me that a policeman who had worked the accident wanted to see me. I walked down the hall, past the coffee machine, and the policeman gave me back Grant's driver's license and told me that the accident was caused by Grant's driving too fast. He also told me something else that I already knew: The station wagon was a total loss.

Yes, Grant was driving too fast. But how fast is too fast? I asked the policeman. He didn't know, he said. "but it was too fast. It happens every once in a while with these young kids. I really hope that he's learned his lesson."

"Had my son been drinking?"

"Sir, there's no evidence of that."

He looked me straight in the eyes when he said that, and my reaction was a sense of relief. I knew that he was telling me the truth. In Grant's room Verna and I kissed him good-night by bending around the traction gear that held his right leg two feet above the bed. He didn't respond—because he was either asleep or sedated into unconsciousness. We left the hospital at six thirty, and I drove Verna home—back to what used to be *our* home. Would I like to come in for some coffee? No, I needed to go back to my place to sleep. I was drained, so very tired that I didn't stir until four in the afternoon, when the telephone cried in my ear.

It was Pop, calling from Missouri. He had heard about the accident—somehow. I told him what the night had been like and tried to comfort him with the physician's optimistic forecast about Grant's recovery. He said that he had prayed that there would be no permanent damage. Then he paused, and I sensed that he was groping for the right words to tell me whatever he had in mind.

"Do you think," he finally began, "that the accident had anything to do with your leaving? Do you think that . . ."

I felt my face flush. In the space of a split second I had become furious, and my voice reflected it: "No, dammit, no! Don't try to lay that on me. I already feel bad enough. Grant drove that car into the tree; I didn't."

Pop's response was calm and reasoned. "Well, I was just wondering if he had so much on his mind that he wasn't paying attention to his driving. I wasn't blaming you. I really wasn't."

"I'm sorry, Pop. I didn't mean to blow off at you. It's been a bad time for me."

"It's been a bad time for everybody. Go back to sleep now. We love you."

"I love you too, Pop."

The next Monday the newspaper carried a story about the accident—because the city editor insisted on it—and a reporter I had hired a year before interviewed me for the parent's perspective. A week later I wrote a column about the accident and described the lessons that I, as a father, felt that I had learned.

—I didn't know my son as well as I thought I did. I always was certain that he was capable of doing things that wouldn't get my approval, but I never thought that using bad judgment in a 4,485-pound station wagon was among them.

Lesson: Never assume that your child is too smart to exercise bad judgment.

—I never understood why auto insurance companies stick it to fathers when teenage sons come of driving age. That's when the insurers jack up premiums to what always seemed to me to be unrealistic levels. When an agent told me that it was because, statistically, the teenage male driver is more accident prone than anybody else, I wanted to argue.

Lesson: Don't argue with statistics.

—I discovered that in a crunch my faith turned to putty. The prayer that I wanted to release as I drove to the accident scene was: "Thy will be done." But the words lodged in my throat. All I could pray was: "Oh, God, please don't let him be dead when I get there. Oh, God, please don't let him be paralyzed." When the heat was on, I was saying: "OK, God, this is one time when I, better than you, know what's best."

Lesson: It's easier for me to leave things in the Lord's hands when the current is going with me, rather than against me.

—I know now that the world is full of people who care about other people and who are motivated primarily by their desire to be compassionate and helpful. For every caller who was "positive" that Grant had been drinking and that the police and I had conspired to cover it up, dozens and dozens of callers said what amounted to: "We want you to know that we're praying for Grant's recovery." Many of the messages came from people whose names I didn't even know.

Lesson: People are beautiful.

Grant was in the hospital for eight weeks, and I visited him every night and almost every lunchtime and, in the beginning, we didn't talk much because he didn't seem to want to talk. Mostly we watched television—*Laverne and Shirley,* the winter Olympic Games, college basketball, *All in the Family.*

"Grant, is there anything I can get for you?"

"What I'd really like is a McDonald's quarter-pounder with cheese and a chocolate milk shake. Do you think you could . . ."

When I returned, I sat in a corner and watched him devour the meal, like a starved cat. "I can't believe a hamburger can taste so good," he said. "Could you bring me another one tomorrow?"

I pulled my chair to the end of the bed and rubbed his feet because, next to hamburgers, that's what he enjoyed most of all. He seldom complained about his discomfort—even if I asked.

"You doing all right?"

"Not bad for somebody who's busted up. But if I never see another bedpan, it'll be all right with me."

I wondered if it was too soon to ask him about the accident. What really had happened?

"Can you remember much about the accident?"

"I was going too damn fast . . . and I started skidding in the loose gravel right off the pavement, and I couldn't control the car. I was hitting mailboxes . . .

and heading straight for the tree. That's all I remember. Somebody told me later that I opened the door, got out of the car, and fell down, but I don't know if that's true."

Grant seemed matter-of-fact about it, as candid as is possible for anybody to be.

"How fast were you going?"

"I don't know—but I was acting like a smart kid, trying to show off, I guess. If I look for a positive side of all of this, I can say that I've learned a lesson—a very valuable lesson . . . What I learned was not to try to show off in a car. I'll be a better driver now—I really will. I'll be more cautious."

I asked him if he knew how fortunate he and David were, and he nodded slightly. "I don't feel like a smart kid anymore. I feel lucky."

"Pop Sifford telephoned and asked about you right after the accident, and—" I stopped. Was this the time to ask Grant if he had been so troubled by my leaving that he took a chance and almost killed himself? No, this wasn't the time. That would have to be asked later, much later.

"Pop called?" Grant's face brightened. "What did he say?"

"He said he had prayed that you weren't badly hurt and that you'd recover quickly."

"I want to write him a letter . . . and tell him not to worry."

Every evening, when I left, Grant thanked me for visiting. "It's important to know that you'll be here." But he also always asked me to leave early if school friends telephoned from the lobby to announce that they were on the way up. "I feel more comfortable if you're not here when they come. I hope you understand."

I told him that I did understand—even though I didn't. "Yeah, sure . . . I've got to be going anyway. I still have a batch of newspapers to go through tonight to get ready for tomorrow."

What was happening, although at the time I didn't know it, was that I was getting my basic training for what would follow in the course of our many-months-long struggle to become father and son again—not as we had been before, but better, in a different, adult kind of way. The key, I would discover, was not to push too hard, not to try to force myself on him. Instinctively, in the hospital, that's what I did, although so many times I found myself quietly wishing: If he'd just let me stay . . .

Verna came to the hospital every day, too, often from early morning until late afternoon, and our visits usually overlapped. The conversation, for my part, was uncomfortable, and I sensed that it was for her, too. She never asked me to come back home, but I read it between the lines of everything she said—which probably told more about me than about her. Mostly we talked about Grant and tried to bring him into the conversation. He, too, seemed ill at ease with a situation that at best felt contrived. More and more, it occurred to me, he was repeating, "Boy, I'll really be glad to get out of here"—and my thought was that he wanted to escape from us as much as the hospital.

One day in the hall, outside Grant's room, Verna told me that he had asked her a question through the drug-induced haze that lingered across the first weekend. He had asked, she said, "Now will Daddy come home?"

"I don't want to hear that," I said acidly.

"Why not?"

"Because I don't believe it."

But that night, as I lay sobbing in bed, I found that I did believe it. The pain that I felt came from two sources—the reality that he had asked the question and the certainty with which, in some way, I would have to answer, "No, Daddy's not coming home."

Chapter 11

From Darkness,
a Flicker Becomes a Flame

The letter was typed, and for that I was thankful—because somehow I was able to imagine fleetingly that the words were coming from Jay's fingers and not from his heart. As I read, I first was stunned. Then I was angry. And finally I was crushed—flattened by emotional pain that flooded through my upper body and emerged as tears that I thought never would cease to flow.

"Dear Darrell:

"That's the only way I can think of you now—as Darrell. I never again can think of you as my father . . . Not ever again. When you love somebody, as you have said you love us, you don't do what you have done. You don't stop sending us money every month—as you promised you would. You don't put me in a position where I have to write to the bank manager and tell him that he should go ahead and repossess my car because I can't make the payments any longer and because the man who once was my father apparently won't make the payments anymore.

"I don't know how anybody can do to other people what you have done to us—not even to strangers, let alone people you profess to love and with whom you

182

lived for so many years. I'm not sure that I ever want to see you again, but I am sure of one thing: I don't want you to write to me; I don't want you to telephone me; I don't want you to contact me in any way. It is possible, I suppose, that my feelings will change as time passes, although I doubt it. If I want to contact you, I will. Otherwise this is good-bye. I wish I could tell you that I love you, but in honesty I cannot."

He hadn't even signed the letter. Instead, at the bottom he had typed: "Sincerely, Jay."

I sat on the couch, numb and fearful, and alternately folded, unfolded, and refolded the letter. I would read it again—yes, that's what I would do. Perhaps I had only imagined the horror of it all. No, it was real. I didn't want to read it again . . . ever. Oh, Jay, if you only understood . . . No, you'll never understand. Well, that's OK. Dammit, that's OK. I can be a whole person without you—and without Grant, too, if it comes to that. If you don't want me as your father, that's all right. It's your choice—and I'll survive!

I dropped the letter to the thin, hard, cheap carpet on the apartment floor, but then I immediately retrieved it. No, Jay, I didn't mean that. I'm not sure I can make it if I'm forever cut off from you and Grant. Jay, please, believe me: I didn't mean what I said! I care about you . . . I really do.

I was hysterical, out of control, and my world was crashing down around me. How could anybody, if he loved his children, do what I had done—reduce the money to them to a trickle? Yes, the lawyer had said that it would be cold, brutal, and cruel, but he also had said that it would be effective in getting a financial settlement that I could live with ... after eighteen months of negotiations that had brought us absolutely nowhere. As I sat there in the chill of the air conditioner's blast, I felt cold and clammy—not from the outside but from within.

* * * * *

It was almost a year earlier that I had sprawled out on the orange-and-cream sofa in my office at *The Charlotte News*. Usually I closed the door when I reclined, but on this day I didn't. Beyond my open door was Tina Robertson, my secretary, who registered mock surprise at my position. She smiled warmly, help up her coffee cup, and mouthed the words, "You want some coffee?"

I shook my head. She went back to her work and I returned to my thoughts. Here I was, at age forty-five, in the kind of job that I believed I had always wanted. I was executive editor of a newspaper of which I was proud—at least much of the time. I liked the staff that we had assembled over the years, people who in some ways were like us, the editors, people who took the business seriously, who displayed pride in their work, who shared the agonies and the triumphs, who often went the extra mile when it was beyond reason for them to do so. Yet in one important way I felt that they were different from me: they went home at night, I imagined, and turned loose of it all, laughed with their children and made love with their mates. When I went home at night, I couldn't turn loose—not even when I was in the suburbs with Jay and Grant and the woman who was my wife. Being an editor was—because I had made it so—a 24-

hour-a-day job with time for not much else, including myself.

Once, I remembered, Grant had come through the newsroom with his junior high school journalism class, and he had stuck his head into my office, smiled, and said, "Hi, Dad." Some of his classmates had gathered around the door, and one of them had asked Grant: "Is he really your father? What does he do?" Grant's smile had faded and he had answered dryly, "Mostly he works."

Another time, when he had come with me to the office on a Saturday morning, he had surveyed the orange draperies that coordinated with the sofa and the orange stuffed chairs and remarked, "Hey, this really is nice."

"Would you like to have an office like this someday?"

"No, I don't believe so."

"What do you mean—you don't believe so? Why not?" Strangely, I had felt threatened and even a little irate.

"Well," Grant had begun, with a smile dancing across his face, "I know what you had to do to get here and what you have to do to stay here. I just don't think a job—any job—ever could be that important to me." He had paused, as if waiting for me to respond but, when I didn't, he had continued, "Is it really *that* important to you?"

I had felt my face flush—and it must have shown too—because Grant had turned away, fearful that he had asked one question too many. "Yes, Grant, it is *that* important to me. And someday, if you're lucky, you'll have a job that is *that* important to you, too. I

hope so, anyway, because that's what separates people who make it from people who don't. The people
who make it have jobs that are important to them."

Now, as I got up from the sofa to close the door,
those words from so long ago sneered mockingly at
me. No job was worth everything—and everything
was what I had put into this job for what seemed
much of my lifetime. I pushed the door softly until it
clicked shut, and then I went back to the sofa and
asked myself why I had honored work more than—I
winced in grief at the very thought— more than
myself and the people I loved.

Why?

Suddenly the answer thundered into my consciousness—perhaps in the same way that a drowning man's
life is supposed to flash across his mind. I chuckled
at the grim analogy that I had conjured up, but I
knew, at some level, that I was drowning—not in
water but in the work ethic to which I had bound
myself.

I had honored work for what seemed to be three
separate but related reasons. The first: To prove, in
the early years, that I could be successful and wipe
out what I viewed as the football stigma. After all, if I
became a newspaper editor, nobody could say that I
was a loser and a quitter. The second: To establish, in
the middle years, that I had excelled beyond my
father's ability to grasp and that I was not and never
would be in a situation in which the world could do to
me what it had done to him. The third: To disguise, in
the later years, the dreadful truth that being an editor
wasn't as fulfilling as I had expected it to be. If I
buried myself in work, I didn't have to come to grips

with that—and I didn't have to ask, What's wrong with me?

I was the classic workaholic who, when he found that his life lacked zest, thought that the remedy must be to work even harder and longer. It was a textbook case of gamesmanship, but the difficulty was that I was playing the game against myself and thus I could not win. I could only lose and drag down not only myself but also Jay and Grant. What example was I setting for them? I didn't want to deal with that at the moment, but I had no choice. It was there before me, so horrifyingly clear: By word and deed, I was telling Jay and Grant that, on the one hand, work was all that mattered but that, on the other hand, work didn't bring happiness. Was I condemning them to the same kind of occupational lunacy that had clutched me for so long?

At age forty-five I had to ask myself a question that I should have grappled with at twenty-two: What did I want out of life?

The dialogue coursed through my mind.

"I want to be happy. That's what I want out of life."

"Well, what would it take to make you happy?"

"I don't know. Dammit, I don't know. Can't you see that's why I'm struggling so?"

"Come on now. Think about it. What do you need?"

"Maybe I can come at it from the other end—by talking about what I *don't* need."

"OK, let's try that. What don't you need?"

"I don't need a job that's not fun, a job that causes me to look forward too much to weekends and not enough to Mondays. I don't need a job that causes me to play games with myself."

"Well, how do you get out of that box?"

"I change jobs."

"Fine, fine. It took you long enough to figure that out. What do you most enjoy about what you're doing now?"

"The writing. The column writing. If I didn't have that, everything else would be unbearable. If I had to sit and juggle papers and sign travel vouchers like a lot of editors, I couldn't survive. One of two things would happen to me."

"Like what?"

"Either I'd be a scratch golfer or I'd be an alcoholic. Those would be the escape routes for me—the golf course or the bottle. But with the writing, well, at least I could tolerate some of the boring stuff because I could get my stimulation from the people I interviewed and the columns I wrote."

"Haven't you pretty much answered the question now about what you want out of life?"

"What do you mean?"

"You're not an editor; you're a writer. You want to be a full-time writer. What's holding you up?"

"How—how can I give up all of this, what I've worked for all these years? What would people say? I know what they'll say: 'He's a failure; he wasn't good enough.' I'm not sure I'm ready for that."

"Does it really matter what anybody else thinks? Isn't the important thing that you be happy? Come on . . . say it."

"Yes, that's right. The important thing is to do what needs to be done to get things in order. I did that when I broke up the marriage, didn't I? And I wasn't overly concerned about what people would think, was I? Do you think I could be happy again as a writer?"

"If I were in your shoes, I'd find out. Come on . . . do it."

"OK, I will. And thanks."

"For what?"

"For helping me confront myself."

I stood up, stretched, and marveled at the value of talking to myself. Then I walked to the window and looked out across Charlotte's Church Street, where the view consisted of a parking garage and an abandoned potato chip factory. No, it wouldn't be hard to give *that* up. But in candor I had to admit that what would be difficult would be surrendering the amenities—the trappings of success that went with an editor's position. I would not only have to turn loose of the private office and the washroom and all of that, but I would have to shoulder the nitty-gritty details of daily life, too—the things that Tina Robertson had done for me for so many years. Let's see now. How long had it been since I'd arranged my own hotel accommodations and reserved a rental car at the airport?

I mentally replayed part of an interview from the year before with General William Westmoreland, who had retired from the Army, come home to South Carolina and built on Charleston's Tradd Street a grand two-story residence into which he had shoehorned the mementos of a lifetime. He had shown me the house, but then he had taken me out back to the guest cottage, and we had talked there . . . for hours . . . not only about how his life had been but also about how his life was now.

I had liked him immensely right from the beginning, and I sensed that he trusted me enough to drop his guard and come at me with straight talk. The toughest thing about not being a general anymore, he said, was that he had to learn to do for himself what others always had done for him—things such as direct dialing long-distance telephone calls and making his own airplane reservations. It had been so terribly confusing, he said. "You know, I think that one of the proudest moments of my life was when I discovered that I could do things for myself . . . It was like I had become part of the world again—like everybody else."

I turned away from the view of the potato chip factory and allowed that if General Westmoreland could do it, I surely could do it, too. Within an hour the telephone call was placed to Detroit to the vice-president in charge of news for Knight-Ridder Newspapers, Inc., the parent company of *The Charlotte News* and forty or so other newspapers across the country. Two days later the vice-president appeared in Charlotte and, over dinner, asked me what I wanted to do.

"I want to be a columnist for somebody."

"That's what I hoped you'd say. How'd you like to go to Philadelphia?"

Suddenly my throat felt dry, and I reached for my glass of bourbon and water.

Of all the cities in the corporate network, Philadelphia was one of the few that I had never considered on those rare occasions when I had wondered what it would be like to live and work in various places.

What were the other cities I never considered? At the moment I wasn't sure, but I thought later that they must have been Grand Forks, North Dakota, and Gary, Indiana. I had been to Philadelphia three or four times for editors' meetings, and it seemed a pleasant-enough place, but I was haunted by the memory of a friend who had left The Associated Press in the Carolinas and gone to work in public relations for Temple University's medical school. In less than a year he had quit and reclaimed his old job with AP, explaining to me one day as he pulled a fifth of Scotch from his golf bag, "Philadelphia's big and dirty and awful."

I recalled the night that we had given a farewell party for the newspaper's general manager, who had been transferred to Philadelphia to head business operations for the newly acquired *Philadelphia Inquirer*. He had accepted our good wishes and reminded us that W. C. Fields allegedly had had carved on his tombstone: "On the whole, I'd rather be in Philadelphia." I had laughed louder than anybody, but now, suddenly, it didn't seem funny anymore.

But I needed a change, and, yes, I was ready to move on. Within forty-five days I would be a columnist for *The Philadelphia Inquirer*. I didn't know then that it would be the best move of my life, both personally and professionally. But before that could happen, a river of turbulent water would wash over the dam and gush under the bridge.

* * * * *

Jay and Grant accepted the news of my transfer without any outward displays of emotion or surprise.

"Do you *have* to go?" Jay asked.

191

"It's something I need to do, yes," I told him.

"OK, but I hope you're certain."

Grant said that he wished the newspaper hadn't printed a front-page story about my leaving.

"Why?"

"Because some of my friends now are asking me if I'm going to Philadelphia, too."

"Does that bother you?"

"It's just something I'd rather not think about."

The woman who still legally was my wife told me that she had not relinquished hope that reconciliation was possible. Neither had the children, she said.

"How do you know that?" I asked.

"I heard Grant up in his room the other day. You know how messy his room always is, how he never cleans up anything. Well, he was there in his room, sorting out what he wanted to keep from what he wanted to throw away."

"Why?"

"He said he was getting ready to move to Philadelphia. He said he just knew that we all were going to be together again."

That night I couldn't sleep a wink. How do you tear to shreds the dream of a boy you love? Do you tell him—or do you not? I decided that I wouldn't confront him with the impossibility of his dream. No, I would wait, for better or for worse, and later, perhaps, he would come to terms with his own reality.

I departed for Philadelphia in my four-year-old Opel GT with two hundred dollars in my pocket and a lump in my chest. The lump was caused, not by the uncertainty of what awaited me in Philadelphia but by the certainty of what I left behind in Charlotte.

On the very first day in Philadelphia I bought a Flyers' sweat shirt for Jay and a Phillies' T-shirt for Grant and put them in the mail along with a letter in which I wrote:

"This is the beginning of a new kind of life for me—writing on a big newspaper and being away from the two of you. I miss you, and I hope that I can see you again soon."

At first their letters arrived frequently and with the flavor of curiosity and enthusiasm. What was Philadelphia *really* like? Could I send them a picture of the apartment building where I lived? Did it have a swimming pool? Was I close to a golf course? How long did it take me to drive to the office?

I answered each of their questions, but my efforts to get information from them fell short. How was school? "It's OK." What had they been up to? "Not much." As the months slipped past, their letters became less frequent and more reserved, and it was obvious that more than distance was coming between us. What I needed was a trip to Charlotte to see them. But how? What would I do—stay in a hotel and invite them up to my room? That would serve only to exaggerate the strangeness of our situation, I feared. No, I needed something better than that.

What I needed was . . .

The telephone demanded my attention early one morning, and it was a Charlotte accountant who once had heard me speak to his Rotary Club. He was program chairman for an association of accountants along the Eastern seaboard, and they were holding their annual meeting in Pinehurst, the storybook-beautiful golfing capital of the nation, which lay like a diamond in North Carolina's sandhills country not far from the Fort Bragg military reservation. Would I be willing to appear on the program? They didn't have a fat fee for me, but they would pay my expenses and, if I wanted to bring anybody with me, they would absorb those expenses, too.

It was like the answer to a prayer. I would fly to Charlotte, rent a car, pick up Jay and Grant, and then the three of us would share a long weekend in Pinehurst. It would be the perfect setting for a reunion, for talking about what was on our minds. It would be like it used to be. No, a thousand times no! It would be so much better than it used to be . . . because I was changing. They would see, surely, that I was beginning to mellow, that I loved them very much, that their happiness mattered to me. Surely . . .

If the trip weren't a disaster, it came close. At the very least it demonstrated clearly how far apart we had drifted and how much ground had to be made up if we ever were to have a relationship that would be satisfying to any of us. Jay and Grant agreed reluctantly to accompany me, but it seemed that their coming together was more to insulate themselves against me than to be with me. We walked together through the pine forests and we talked about the incredible natural beauty, but it was as if a shield kept us apart. I could have tried harder to penetrate the shield, but I didn't. I didn't want to back them into a corner from which they might feel a need to fight their way to freedom.

We drove back to Charlotte in relative silence.

They seemed apprehensive and I felt frightened and hurt, almost like a little boy rather than a father. I wanted to grab them and cry: "I love you! Please tell me that you love me, too! Please tell me that you accept what I've done—even if you don't understand why I did it!" I wanted to, but I didn't. When you feel frightened and hurt, in a little boy's way, you can't do much of anything—except try to pretend that your heart doesn't ache and that your eyes are misty, not from sadness but from the sun's glare through the windshield.

We arrived at the mustard-colored house in the suburbs, and I pulled into the driveway where Sherman, the basset hound, and Allie, the black cat, played their forever game of bite, scratch, and run. I parked the car, got down on my knees, and scratched Sherman behind the ears and rolled Allie on his back and stroked his stomach—our ancient ritual.

I turned to Jay and Grant to say "Hey, look, they remember," but Jay and Grant already had gone inside the house. And it was time for me to get back to Philadelphia.

* * * * *

The letters from my lawyer in Charlotte arrived once or twice a month, and without exception all of them told the same story: The financial negotiations that were a necessary prelude to a formal separation agreement and then divorce were mired down in disagreement. The reason for the disagreement was classic: She wanted more than I felt that I could afford to pay—and have anything left for myself. Through her lawyer, whose fees I had agreed to pay, she wanted not only money now but a guarantee that she forever would share in a percentage of salary increases and income from outside writing, including book royalties.

If I couldn't agree to this, then we'd just have to go to court and let a judge decide, she said. It would be nice if we could settle this like two intelligent people, but if push came to shove . . .

I asked my lawyer if I likely would benefit or suffer if the case went to court.

"I can't tell you that. It depends to a large degree on which judge you'd get."

"You think I should give her what she's asking? It's not reasonable, is it?"

"No."

"What should *we* do?"

"I know what *I* would do. I'd cut back on the money. Just tell her that you can't afford the voluntary payments."

It sounded like a broken record to me—the same thing I'd heard that day in his office so many months ago. My response sounded like a broken record too: "I don't see how I can do that—without starving out the kids. It's not possible, is it?"

"No. You'd have to take your chances. But it's up to you. Just tell me what you're going to do before you do it."

"I don't think I can do that to the kids . . ."

A week later a copy of another letter arrived from her lawyer. More money, more demands, more guarantees.

I dialed my lawyer at his home. "Eddie, I'm ready to do it."

"OK. My experience is that this will give us the

kind of leverage that's needed to speed up things."

"Eddie, tell me that my kids won't hate me."

"I wish I *could* tell you that. But what I can tell you is that even if they do hate you now, they won't always hate you. They really won't. That's my experience."

"I want very much to believe you."

With the money reduced to a trickle, the telephone lines began to heat up—from Charlotte to Philadelphia.

First it was Jay: "Hey, we don't have any money. What's going on?"

Then it was Grant: "It seems like I haven't had a good meal in a long time. What's happening?"

And then she was on the line: "How do you expect us to live?"

The conversations tied me in knots—not because they were painful, which they were, but because I couldn't be honest in what I said. The answer to "What's going on?" had to be, "Well, money's getting really tight up here, and I can't pay anywhere near as much as I used to pay." It wasn't prudent to say—because of the legal games that must be played—that I was willing to starve them out, if I had to, to get some action started on a settlement that seemed reasonable for all of us.

Yes, of course, I would pay for their college educations, but I couldn't even assure them of that—because the gamesmanship got in the way.

What were Jay and Grant thinking about me? Did they hate me as much as I feared they might?

I hurried to the mailbox, as I did every day, hoping that the mail would yield a letter from Jay or Grant but knowing full well that it would not. To my surprise there was a letter—with Jay's name as the return address. I ripped open the envelope and found not one letter but two. Could it be that both Jay and Grant had written to me? No, the reality was that neither had written to me. One of the letters was from a bank manager who told Jay that unless his car payments were made current, the car would be repossessed—the canary yellow Opel GT that I had helped him pick out a year before. The other letter was a copy of what Jay had written back to the bank manager: "I guess you'll have to take my car because my father won't send us the money for the payments—like he promised. He cares so little about us that he doesn't care if you take my car . . ."

It was a letter that seemed deliberately written to wound me, and in anger I started to telephone Jay. No, it's better to wait . . . until the passion has subsided. OK, now for the call.

"Jay, I'm not going to let them take your car away from you. Believe me, that won't happen."

"We don't have any money." His voice was icy.

"Jay, you'll keep the car . . ."

A week later the other letter arrived:

"Dear Darrell:

"That's the only way I can think of you now—as Darrell. I never again can think of you as my father . . ."

Oh, how it hurt, but the financial squeeze was generating activity. The proposals and counterproposals from the lawyers were narrowing the differences. Finally, there was one that I thought I could live with. I didn't like it, but I could manage it.

"Eddie, can we go with this one?"

"No, it's still too much. We can do better. Just hold off a while longer. I know it hurts, but hold off. Will you?"

Then he called me. "OK now, we've reached the point where we can do business. You're going to have a settlement very soon . . . and then we'll arrange for the divorce. When can you come to Charlotte?"

"What for?"

"For the divorce. You have to appear in court yourself."

Outside the courtroom I stood in the corridor, fidgeted with the lapels of my gray-flannel suit, and focused on the others who were waiting to get inside for their day—or brief moment—in court.

Mostly they were women, middle-aged, who seemed almost absurd in their efforts to appear lighthearted:

"Yes, this is it. In just a few minutes I'll be single again. Isn't it exciting?"

"Wow, single after all these years. Can you imagine what it'll be like?"

"It's not the end of a marriage; it's the start of a new life."

My lawyer's associate was beside me, telling me that the judge would ask me if I had filed for the divorce, when we had married, when we had separated, how many children I had, if I had made financial arrangements to support my children.

"That's all?" I asked.

"Yes, that's all," the lawyer said. "It's just a formality."

By my watch it took one minute and nineteen

seconds to dissolve legally a marriage that had struggled along for almost twenty-two years. Then a court clerk gave me a form document that had been dated and signed by the judge. It was the divorce decree—a simple-looking piece of paper that contained not more than fifty words.

Legally the battle was finished, and it was with a profound sense of relief that I walked from the courthouse to a neighboring park with a fountain that gushed a 20-foot-high mountain of water through which the sun painted a rainbow against the Carolina-blue sky.

Grant was there, waiting for me to keep the luncheon date that I had proposed and that he had accepted warily. I waved at him and he walked around the fountain, smiled faintly, and asked,

"Well, it's all over finally, isn't it?"

"Yes. How do you feel?"

"Relieved, I guess. At least now I know where everybody stands. There's something to be said for that."

"How's Jay?"

"He hasn't said much about you or the divorce. But I think he would have come to lunch with us if he didn't have to work."

"You really think so?"

"I think he's tired of the battle. Hell, we're all tired. You, too, I imagine."

"Yeah, me too. You going to come to Philadelphia to visit one of these times? I hope you will."

"I'm not sure I'm ready for that yet."

"What about Jay?"

"I'm pretty sure he's not ready for it."

In the months after Jay's "Dear Darrell" letter to me, I had honored his demand that I not try to contact him. But then I had received a letter from Pop, who in what would be the last year of his life was trying with all his might to bring about a reconciliation between me and the boys.

"I have talked with Jay," his letter began, "and I think that he has heard some of what I said. I'm not sure he wanted to listen, but he and I always have had a special relationship and I think that he listened out of respect for that. I tried to explain that in every marriage that fails there are two sides and that one side usually does not bear every bit of the responsibility. I believe that he would be receptive to talking to you now, but I'm not sure that he'll take the first step. I think that you should call him. I've done everything that I can do to try to fix things between the two of you, and the rest is up to you. But I want you to know that I'd not be happy if you didn't follow through on this. It's too important—for all of us."

In all of our years it was the closest that Pop had come in my adult life to giving me a direct order. I had telephoned Jay that same day and told him about the letter from Pop.

His voice was not warm, but neither did it sound angry. "I'm sorry about what I wrote in that letter. I didn't really mean it that way. I was confused and hurt then. I'm still confused and hurt, but I'm past the point of trying to hurt you. Nothing can come out of hurt except more hurt."

"Can we start writing to each other again?"

"Yes, I think we can. That would be all right."

"Is there anything I can do for you?"

"No, nothing that's possible for you to do."

"What do you mean?"

"Can you make it stop hurting?"

* * * * *

I married Marilyn Oakley, the daughter of a North Carolina tobacco farmer, in the chambers of a federal district court judge in Philadelphia. The judge's wife was the only other person there to witness the three-minute ceremony after working hours on a Thursday afternoon. When it was over, she uncorked a bottle of champagne, and then we went out for dinner. The next morning Marilyn caught the train for her job as a training consultant in the heart of the city, and I drove thirty miles to Lancaster to deliver the luncheon speech at a meeting of the Pennsylvania Press Association.

When I got back to the apartment, I wrote two letters—one to Pop and Mom and the other to Jay and Grant, explaining that I had remarried. To Jay and Grant I wrote that Marilyn was a woman they would like immediately and, I was sure, love eventually. To Pop and Mom I wrote that this marriage, unlike the first, was for all the right reasons. I asked for their support.

Marilyn was not yet thirty when I first met her, a bright, career-conscious woman whose jobs had taken her from being a truant officer for the Raleigh public schools, right out of college, to work in North Carolina state government, to the personnel department of the newspapers in Charlotte, which was where we connected.

She never had been married, not because she hadn't had opportunities but because she had wanted to do the things that single people can do and should do. Eventually, she would marry, she said, if the right man came along, but if he didn't, that would be OK, too. She wasn't about to compromise her standards and settle for less than she wanted. She was, in all ways, a woman whose appeal was strong to me in mid-life but who would have terrified me in my earlier years. She was strong and independent— qualities that I now prized but that, in my twenties, would have caused me to run for my life. Back then I needed a cheerleader, somebody who could give me the support that I couldn't give to myself. But now I needed somebody who could challenge me, when it was appropriate, and support me, too.

In the beginning I amused, baffled, and terrorized her with my drumfire of questions about who she was, where she came from, and what she wanted out of life. After our first lunch she composed herself and told me: "I feel like I've been interviewed for an hour. Is this the way you always act?" No, I said, but it's the way I always act around people in whom I'm very interested. By the third lunch I told her that I thought we had the potential for an everlastingly solid relationship, and by the fifth lunch she gave signs of agreeing with me. "One of the things I like about you," she said, "is that I never have to try to figure out where you stand; you always tell me."

Pop telephoned as soon as he received my letter about marrying Marilyn. "I can't say that I'm not surprised, but you do have our support. You'll always have our support . . . because we love you. Don't ever doubt that."

Two weeks after we were married, Marilyn and I

went to Missouri to meet Pop and Mom, and she made no effort to conceal her uneasiness. "I don't know what it will be like for them—meeting their son's *second* wife," she said. "They seemed to respond all right to your divorce and they sounded positive about your remarriage over the telephone, but how do you think they *really* feel?"

I told Marilyn that they would find her as delightful as I did. "They'll like you because you're likable, but let's be honest: we're not kids, and we don't *need* their approval. It would be nice, but we don't need it."

We drove 125 miles west from St. Louis airport to their house, parked, and walked hand in hand to the front door. I knocked, and we waited, not speaking but instead studying each other's eyes. Then the door opened and there was Pop, his hair more gray, his shoulders more stooped than I had remembered.

"Hi, Pop," I smiled. "This is Marilyn."

Pop started to take her hand, but Marilyn bent forward and kissed him on the cheek. "Hello, Pop," she said. "I've heard so much about you . . . and most of it's been good." She was grinning. Pop grinned back and seemed momentarily at a loss for words. Then he called excitedly: "Mom! Mom! They're here—Darrell and Marilyn!"

Mom appeared—her hair neatly in place and her eyes sparkling through her rimmed spectacles. "Why, yes, Marilyn, come in, won't you? And make yourself at home—because that's how we want you to feel, like you're at home."

It had taken less than a minute, and already the tension was gone. The visit would last for six days and on our final night we would sit on the floor and tape our conversation—perhaps because all of us sensed that this might be our last time together, which it was.

The tape, since Pop's death, is a treasured possession, the only recording of his voice, and once or twice a year, even now, I take it out and play it—usually when I'm alone at night, when Marilyn is on a business trip.

On the tape Pop's voice is weak in volume but forceful in conviction: "Marilyn, you don't know how much it means to Mom and me for you to come to see us. I've never seen Darrell so relaxed and happy. I think you've already added twenty years to his life. He told us from the very beginning that you were a wonderful person, and we can see that you are. We love you—just as we'd love our own daughter. You're special to us, not because you're married to our son but because of the person you are."

* * * * *

The visit with Pop and Mom was rewarding for all of us, especially for Marilyn. All that remained now was for us to hear from Jay and Grant. I didn't expect a telephone call, but surely a letter would arrive shortly.

I waited, and each day I unlocked the mailbox in eager anticipation that their letter would come tumbling out. But it never did.

Chapter 12

Keeping the Door Open

Jay and Grant were keeping their distance, emotionally as well as geographically, and with frightening intensity I began to wonder: Is it always going to be this way? Then almost immediately I shifted to another question: Does it have to be this way? Wasn't there something I could do—something more than write letters that brought not return mail but unbroken silence? Wasn't there a way to keep Jay and Grant from shutting the door on me?

I sought out psychiatrist Henri Parens, whose answer was not without hope: To keep the door open in the long run, a parent might have to allow the door to be shut temporarily.

"Youngsters do experience divorce as a personal affront, a rejection, whether they are young or older," Parens said. "It was quite common ten years ago to say: 'Get a divorce and the kids will learn to live with it.' But we know now that it's not that simple. In clinics and in private practice we're seeing lots of damaged kids. The effect of divorce can be very devastating."

Parens stressed that in all instances it was an individual problem and that it was not wise to try to approach all youngsters in the same way. The emotional experiences vary, but at some point a child may *need* to reject a parent. It's important then for the parent not to counterreject the child.

Parens talked with me for two hours, and this is the unmistakable message with which I came away:

Children very likely have their own fantasy about why their parents divorced, and the fantasy may be a total distortion of reality. But it's a fantasy that belongs to the children, and the result may be that the children reject and malign their father or mother. The fantasy not infrequently is built on this foundation: The child hears the parents arguing. After all, there is no divorce unless there has been extensive distress and emotional injury. A child at times distorts who is responsible for what—and mentally even may enlarge the injury. The end result can be that the child blames one parent and rejects that parent. That is the bad news, and it can be and usually is crippling to the rejected parent. But the good news is that the child's blaming of one parent is going to be subject to change. At times the child will remember things forgotten; will hear one parent say something that resonates with an experience in the past. And the child may shift blame, reduce blame, or eliminate blame.

It is at this moment that the child who has rejected one parent and tightly closed the door on the relationship may want to reopen the door. But if the parent, understandably hurt by rejection, has shut the door, it may not be possible for the child to reopen it, and this may compound the injury to everybody. It always is hoped that parents will be mature enough not to do this, but, as we all know from what we have read and seen, this is not always the case.

The critical task facing the parent is to be able to allow the door to be reopened. How can this be done? The answer sounds as simple as it is—yet in the simplicity lurks the heartbreak that makes it so terribly difficult for some of us some of the time. In the face of outright hostility or smoldering silence parents need to overtly maintain interest in the child and make it not easy for the child to shut the door in the first place.

It is appropriate for a parent to say to the child: "I know this is difficult for you; it's not a picnic for me either. I know you've pushed me away, but I don't want that. I don't want our relationship to go down the drain because of family difficulties." If a parent allows the door to be shut, it should be only because the parent recognizes at the time that it's the only thing the child can do. But it shouldn't be easy. It's bad enough for the family to break up—without the additional wound of the child's estrangement from a parent.

Even if the door has been shut, the parent can continue to communicate love to the child. If the child won't talk on the telephone, the parent can send a letter. Some children may destroy the letter; others may put it in a drawer and read it later; others may read it immediately, keep it, and reread it later.

It is also important for the parent to *insist* on a relationship with the child but not to *badger* the child about it. Understanding the distinction between insisting and badgering is critical. A parent who *badgers* fails to recognize what the child is feeling. The parent disregards the child's reaction and bangs ahead. A parent who *insists* makes it clear that the parent has a stake in the relationship and is making a claim to it— even if the child resists. But the parent also recognizes that the child may not be able to deliver the emotional goods at this time and make possible the reopening of the relationship.

If this happens, a waiting game necessarily must be played—with the rejected parent's continuing to punctuate the silence with phone calls and letters, reaffirming a commitment to the relationship, but not badgering.

It is difficult to overemphasize the importance of talking as a way of working through all misunderstandings in any relationship, even at the international level. If people are talking, they are not as likely to turn to bombs, literally or figuratively. It is very much as Sigmund Freud said so many years ago: "The person who first threw an invective at an enemy instead of a spear was the starter of civilization."

Talking very likely will facilitate resolution. It may not happen as quickly as we, the parents, would like, but what other options exist? And it's important to accept that nothing may come of it, that the whole thing may break down. If that happens, the parent, to decrease some of the pain, necessarily must come to grips with the reality that it may be a long time—a very long time—before reconciliation. In some instances, although they are very rare, reconciliation may never come—but there always is room for hope that the door will be opened.

Why is it so rare for reconciliation never to become

a reality? Because within most of us there is, resulting from early childhood experiences, a yearning to have a positive relationship with both parents. This is no minor inner striving; rather, it is a very important need—to establish a good love relationship. It really is the human condition to need a love relationship. Many in the mental-health field now deny this, but anybody who has observed young children go up to their parents can see that this need is present. Because of this it's possible to say that this built-in yearning enables most children to overcome most obstacles to relationships with both parents.

Can parents somehow sabotage this yearning? Yes, they can—and often they do. When this happens, it opens the way to a lifetime of conflict for the child whom both parents profess to love.

What form does the sabotage take? Not infrequently it appears as verbal darts thrown by one parent against the other. It's important for everybody to recognize this and for the parent who is not estranged from the child to try to facilitate a reconciliation between the child and the estranged parent. What is said by the parent with whom the child lives can be very damaging or very constructive. It's in the best interests of everybody to be constructive, but often intense loyalty conflicts feed into destructive comments.

One example of this: A mother says to the child: "Your father is so mean to me."

Another example: A father says to the child: "Your mother never loved me or you because she's incapable of loving."

Both statements put tremendous burdens on the

child, and the result can be to intensify loyalty to one parent and to intensify rejection of the other parent. While this may sound trivial in the beginning, it may become a major factor with which everybody must deal in the years to come—if the child permanently rejects one parent.

What happens when permanent rejection occurs? There is considerable likelihood that rejecting a parent with whom there once existed a reasonable relationship will create massive guilt in the child.

The child has rejected the father, let's say, out of anger at the father's hurting the mother who is loved by the child. Yet the child also loves the father, the same father whom the child wants to destroy and never see again. The consequence may be that the child will be saddled with what generally is considered as one of the most important neurotic conflicts of all—hating the parent the child also loves. In psychiatry this is called a "conflict of ambivalence," and it can put a child on a rocky road that extends far into life, perhaps even forever.

Absolutely nothing makes us more guilty than wanting to hurt somebody we love. It was Freud, early in the century, who said that guilt comes from having destroyed or wanting to destroy somebody we love. If one parent elicits rejection of the other parent, it only intensifies the child's inner conflict and guilt. It's not a cutesy psychiatric statement to say: "Don't burden your children with your problems." Somebody who once was married must have thought something of the other person, who can't be all bad. If the person is, then it says something about personal judgment, doesn't it? There must be something of value in the other person, and it's better for the child if parents stress the positive instead of the negative.

In whatever ways possible, parents should communicate to the child: "Look, it's OK with me for you to love your father" or mother. This sounds less difficult than it is for many people. The experience of countless mental health professionals adds up to this: Two civilized adults who love themselves, other people, and their child can become really vicious and unbelievably hurtful to each other. The child witnesses this—often time and time again—because people don't get divorced unless they've been traumatized by each other. It's a horrendous experience all around—and the damage can penetrate to the child's core.

One way to minimize the damage is for parents to endorse each other's assets. There is no guarantee that this will work, that parents who don't poleax each other will help their children adjust totally to divorce. But what can we do except try—and hope?

* * * * *

So there I was, continuing to keep the door open with Jay and Grant—even as it seemed that they forever had slammed it shut and secured it with a dead bolt. I was not without encouragement when I discussed my dilemma with friends, but their encouragement, in a strange way, only seemed to intensify my belief that I was on a road that led to nowhere.

Friends would listen, smile sympathetically, sometimes even pat my hand, and then they would say, almost as if they were reading from a master script: "Yes, it's difficult, but hang in there and keep on doing what you're doing. They're young and eventually they'll come around. Don't give up—and don't get angry."

I heard versions of that so often that I did give up—I gave up discussing it with friends. I also did get angry—not at Jay and Grant but at my friends. What they were telling me wasn't ever going to come true, it seemed. The temptation to back off, to stop writing letters was enormous. So was the temptation to try to fool myself into thinking that reasonable relationships with them were not critically important to me. "OK," I would say to myself, "if that's the way you guys want it, that's how it will be. I really don't give a damn anymore and, besides that, there's nothing else I can do. I've tried; I've really tried." Like all games of self-deceit, it wasn't successful—not even a little bit. I'd give myself what I came to call my "don't care" lecture, but immediately a tiny voice would say to me: "You don't believe that. You *do* care; you care very much."

Yes, I did care very much, but I wasn't sure why. Was it because I felt that Jay and Grant needed a relationship with their father and that without it they would be less than they might have been?

Or was it because I needed a relationship with them? Was it because I feared that without them I'd be less than I might otherwise be? How would I feel about myself if Jay and Grant forever rejected me? How would society look at a father who never made it back with his sons? Was my driving motivation for reconciliation primarily selfish? I wasn't sure then, and I'm not even certain now. But one thing of which I'm certain is this: What my friends told me about hanging in there despite a total lack of encouragement from Jay and Grant was the best advice that I ever received. I did hang in there, all right—not because they had told me to but because it seemed that there was nothing else that I could do. I wrote letters and, although no letters came in return, I wrote more letters.

In my letters I tried to paint a picture of my life in Philadelphia as a columnist and my life with Marilyn. "We often go to the South Jersey shore," I wrote to Grant, who, like me, was passionately fond of sun, surf, sand, and sea gulls. "It's only a 50-minute drive from Philadelphia—unlike Myrtle Beach, which is almost four hours from Charlotte. Marilyn enjoys the shore as much as you and I, and in our long walks, as we wade through the water, we talk about our work and our lives. I find that I'm better able now to integrate work into my life. It's no longer the compulsive, disrupting factor that it was for so many years. I am achieving a life balance that I always needed but that I only recently have recognized the need for."

It was something, I wrote, that I would like to discuss with Grant *when* he came to visit us—not *if* but *when*. I told him that I loved him and Jay very much and that I missed them.

I mailed the letter, and, to my surprise, Grant responded. Yes, he wrote, he *would* like to visit. Could I make the airline reservations and arrange for him to pick up the ticket in Charlotte? Would I pay for the ticket?

I was at the airport to meet him when he walked up the ramp—a slender, bearded young man in a blue denim suit and open-neck sport shirt.

"Hi, stranger," I said. I grasped his hand, hoping desperately that my sweaty palm wouldn't betray my anxiety—but then recognizing that anxiety was a normal reaction to the tension of the meeting.

"Hi," Grant answered. "It's been a long time." His handshake was firm, and his eyes were directly fixed on mine. "You sound as if things are going well for you."

"They are going well, Grant. And for you?"

"Well, uh, yeah. I'm a little uneasy about starting college, but I guess that's normal, isn't it?"

Yes, I told him, it's as normal as a sweaty palm in a long-awaited handshake. He grinned at that, and together we rode the escalator down to the baggage claim carrousel.

The visit, which lasted a week, was splendid even if it wasn't altogether satisfying. Because I was fearful of pushing too hard and trying to make up too much ground too quickly, I held back and didn't say much of what I wanted to say and what, in retrospect, would have been appropriate to say. For his part Grant was tentative in his behavior because, he would say later, he was on strange turf. He didn't know if I'd be the same father, if he'd like Marilyn, if Marilyn would like him.

It was obvious from the beginning that he and Marilyn indeed liked each other. She talked with him, drew him out, and seemed better than I to attribute the occasional long pauses in his conversation to the newness of the situation rather than to his not having much to say to us.

"He's awfully quiet," I complained to Marilyn on the first night.

"I know you've heard this before," she answered, "but give him time. How would you have felt if your parents had divorced and if you had visited your father and his new wife?"

"I probably wouldn't have felt too sure of myself."

"Well, you've just described Grant. But he'll be OK. He's a courageous kid—otherwise he wouldn't be here."

Grant and I drove to the South Jersey shore the third day of the visit and there, as we lay on our chairs in the sand, the first spark of what used to be was rekindled.

"Grant, I left my wallet in the car. Dig the keys out of the beach bag and I'll go get the wallet and we'll have some ice cream."

He dug and dug some more. "I can't find the keys."

I dug, too. The keys were not in the beach bag.

"They must have fallen out into the sand. We're locked out of the car," I said, trying to mask my irritation.

"Well, let's find the keys," Grant said. "They've got to be around here somewhere."

Together, on our knees, almost shoulder to shoulder, we began to comb through the fine, white sand with our fingers. I looked directly into his face and asked, "Does this remind you of anything?"

He grinned wistfully. "It's kind of like plugging in zoysia grass, isn't it? Only it's a lot easier."

At that instant the years evaporated and there I was, back in the suburbs, in the front yard with Grant beside me . . . and with Sherman and Allie biting, scratching, and running. "How does the zoysia grass look these days?" I asked.

"Not as good as it used to," he answered in a matter-of-fact voice. "We don't put in the time on it that you used to."

"Come on; dig faster. We've got to find the car keys."

"Hey! Here they are. I got 'em! I got 'em!" In triumph Grant held aloft the sand-caked key holder. He smiled and I smiled. Nobody said anything else, but both of us understood.

After that visit Grant's letters were more regular—and even Jay began to write occasionally, although his letters were cool, formal, and distant and never contained any reference to Marilyn. It was as if she didn't exist. On the other hand, Grant's letters often mentioned her—and in a fashion that seemed increasingly comfortable for him. My nickname for Marilyn was "M," and Grant quickly picked up on that: "Tell M that I often think about how good her chicken was when I was up there."

The next year Grant came back again—and once more he and I went to the South Jersey shore, this time not to Avalon, where we had lost the car keys, but to Stone Harbor, the quaint village directly south of Avalon, a sleepy little town that is peaceful even at the height of the summer.

There, on a misty afternoon, on a red, white, and blue bench on the northeast corner of 96th and Third Avenue, we sat and talked and shared our thoughts. It was the kind of event that was so meaningful that, even as it unfolded, I knew that it forever would be among my treasured memories.

It had been so long since Grant and I had talked about things beyond baseball, college, cars, and newspapers. But on this day we talked about God, life before death, life after death, marriage, divorce, love, relationships, happiness, despair, the past, the future, the very moment we were experiencing. And we talked about Pop, Grant's grandfather, and about what he had told me not long before his death: Tell the people who are important to you that they are important, that they matter, that you love them. Tell them while they are around you and able to hear what you're saying. Don't put it off—and be too late and so sorry.

As we sat on the bench, I told Grant what I felt: "You matter to me very much." He didn't respond, but he didn't change the subject either. Rather, he allowed the tenderness of the instant to linger until it dissipated on its own.

Then it was time for him to return to North Carolina. We drove to the airport, the three of us. I shook his hand and Marilyn hugged him. Grant told me that he was glad we'd been able to talk so much. He said he was looking forward to coming back next summer. I was about to choke on my Adam's apple. I wanted to hug him—all six feet, four inches of him. But I didn't. I started to, but I stopped and instead grasped his upper arm with my right hand. He hesitated an instant, then he was gone, out the door and into the blue-and-white jetliner.

As Marilyn and I drove back home, we talked about the visit and our expectations of next summer. Then she asked, "You wanted to hug him, didn't you?"

"Yes."

"What stopped you?"

"I was afraid I'd embarrass him. I was afraid he'd say, 'Aw, Darrell, don't do that here in front of all these people.' So I backed off. And I'm sorry. I wish I could do it over again."

Marilyn said that she felt Grant understood, but she added, "I think he was waiting for you to hug him."

The next day I wrote Grant a letter and told him what I had felt, what I had feared—his embarrassment and possible rejection. And I told him that for somebody who thinks that he's open and honest in showing emotion, I really had goofed our good-bye.

I found myself, I told Grant, in the spot that my father had urged me and everybody else to avoid: I was sorry—not for what I had done but for what I had not done. I told him that I wouldn't let it happen again, that next time, if I wanted to hug him, I would—unless he told me not to.

For a long time he didn't respond. Then one day his letter came. He didn't mention what I had written until the end, when he said: "You're very honest in sharing your emotions. I respect that. I really do."

The next summer Grant visited again, and I had on my agenda one item of unfinished business—something from which I had backed off that afternoon in Stone Harbor. I had backed off because I was afraid—afraid that I would be unable to endure Grant's response to it. But now, on this visit, I *had* to do it. I had to tell Grant that I was sorry that I hadn't performed better as a father when he and Jay were little; I was sorry not only for what I had done but also for the many things that I had not done.

For a long time this had crawled around in my

stomach. It was difficult because it wasn't like asking a thirteen-year-old boy to rate me as a father—as I once had done with Jay. Grant was a man, a third-year college student, who knew me as I was back then, when he was growing up and when, as Jay had put it, I had hollered too much, worked too much, played golf too much, fathered too little.

From an adult perspective Grant knew where the skeletons were. He had seen me at my worst. How would he react if I told him I was sorry? Would he tell me that, yes, I had plenty to be sorry for, that I had shortchanged him and left him without the foundation to which every child was entitled? Would he be unable to forgive and forget? It would be, I knew, an occasion when I would bare my ultimate vulnerability to him and await his bite of anger and resentment. I feared it; but I had no choice. It was necessary for me to do it.

We went to New York City—because Grant had never been there and because our beloved Cardinals were in town to play baseball against the Mets. We took the subway to Shea Stadium, where the Cardinals swept a doubleheader as we cheered, drank our beer, and chased foul balls in the nearly deserted park. It was a good start to the visit, I thought, but the hard work was still to come. When would I do it? When *could* I do it?

It happened quite by accident, really, but at a spot that I would have chosen if I had anticipated it: the Algonquin Hotel on West 44th Street, not far off Times Square. It was where I always stayed, if I had a choice, when I was in New York because it held so many pleasant memories for me.

The first time I ever had been at the Algonquin, when I was lecturing at the American Press Institute at Columbia University, I had waited for the elevator in the lobby late at night and when the elevator arrived and the door opened, I was jarred by what I saw. There, standing nonchalantly in the back of the elevator, was Peter Ustinov, the actor. He smiled broadly and announced, "Hi, welcome to the Algonquin."

I didn't know it then, but that's the kind of hotel that the Algonquin is, a place where the famous come to dine, drink, and talk and where their presence is so commonplace that few pay any attention to them. The next morning, at breakfast, I had stared in amazement at the woman sitting alone at the next table—Jean Stapleton, who for so many years portrayed Archie Bunker's wife, Edith, on television's *All in the Family.* She had nodded a polite greeting and resumed her meal. From another table a young woman had approached Miss Stapleton, notebook in hand, eager for her autograph, but a waiter had intercepted her and said discreetly, "We don't do that here." The young woman had retreated in silence, and I wasn't sure that anybody else ever was aware of what had happened—or had not happened. That was how the Algonquin did things, quietly and with style.

The next time I had been at the Algonquin I had been introduced to the Algonquin cat, which would become a legend in its own time because somebody decided to publish a cartoon book titled simply *Algonquin Cat.* The cat had to be seen to be believed, a black-and-white, gregarious creature named Hamlet, who roamed the hotel lobby and carefully greeted each of the guests, who sat, as Algonquin guests usually do, in the stuffed chairs beside the tables with the blazing candles and sipped drinks that were brought by waiters from the tiny Blue Bar near the entrance onto 44th Street.

Because I love cats, the Algonquin cat was a special pleasure to me. Marilyn felt that way, too. She's also a cat person, and on her trips to New York she sometimes went out of her way to stop at the Algonquin and play with the cat. Once when she went into the lobby and couldn't find Hamlet, she asked a waiter where he was. With a deadpan expression the waiter answered: "Well, it's Hamlet's day off. But if you come back tomorrow, he'll be here." That was how the Algonquin did things—with humor and style.

In the blistering heat of an August afternoon, Grant and I stopped at the Algonquin for a drink. He chose a beer and I a gin and tonic and, as we sat in the walnut-paneled bar, I knew that the moment had come. If I didn't do it now, I'd never be able to do it. My D-Day was at hand.

"Grant, I've got something I need to say to you. It's not going to be easy for me to say, and I may falter— or even cry. But please bear with me and listen to me . . . because I have to talk about this. OK?"

He put down his glass and looked expectantly at me.

"I'm listening."

"Grant, what I want to tell you is that I'm sorry that I wasn't better as a father when you and Jay were little. I'm sorry I hollered so much, sorry I spent so many weekends on the golf course when I could have gone fishing with you . . . or to the ice cream store or the movies or the park. I am really sorry . . ." My voice was beginning to crack from the emotion that was swelling my throat, but I plowed on:

"I'd like to be able to go back and try again, but, of course, I can't do that. So I'm doing the only thing that's still possible—I'm asking you to forgive me and accept me now, as I am, rather than as I was. It hurts. It really hurts to look back and realize how poorly I did at the most important job in my life—being a father to you and Jay."

I tried to sip from my gin and tonic, but my hands shook and sloshed it out onto the table. "That's as plain as I can say it to you, Grant. I'm sorry for being the way I was so much of the time. I've mellowed since then, but, dammit, it's come too late to be of much benefit to you and Jay. I'm sorry . . ."

I looked down at the table, unable to bear the fury that I imagined was building in Grant's face. But when I finally looked up, after a moment's silence, I saw not fury but what looked like surprise—and confusion.

"Darrell," he began—that's what he called me now—"you're the only father we ever had and, when you yelled at us, we didn't think anything was wrong. We thought everybody's fathers yelled at them. It was the way it was—and we accepted it, just like we accepted your playing golf and working so much. It was the only life-style we knew."

He was talking softly, but in the intimacy of the Blue Bar, I imagined that the other half dozen patrons could hear every word. But why didn't they turn and look at us? How could they not respond to the drama that was taking place right before them? How could they sit there and drink?

Grant continued: "I know that your job was tough back then. Being an editor would make it difficult for anybody to be mellow. I understand that and I accept that—just as I did back then, when I was little . . . You know, I never really felt ignored. I never felt that you didn't have time for me. Don't you remember all the times we played baseball together and how often you worked with me when I was pitching in Little League? Don't you remember how some of the neighborhood kids used to watch us? They envied me—because their fathers never did *anything* with them. They thought I was lucky—and so did I."

I turned away because I didn't want Grant to see the tears rolling down my face, but then I turned back because I didn't care. He looked at me, smiled faintly, and continued:

"You're being too hard on yourself. You probably weren't the world's greatest father—but whose father is the world's greatest? You did a lot better job than you seem to think. You don't have anything to apologize for. I never felt deprived or unloved. I didn't understand a lot of what you did back then, but I never felt that I couldn't count on you. I always knew that you liked me . . ."

One of the greatest fears of my life had been laid to rest. Through my wet eyes I looked at Grant and said: "Thanks. You're a very big person—bigger than I ever imagined anybody who's gone through what you have could be. Thanks."

"No, I'm not big. If I'm anything, I'm honest. That's all."

We rode the Metroliner back to Philadelphia, and then it was time for Grant to leave for North Carolina. As I looked back on what happened, I realized that if it didn't wipe the slate clean, at least it helped me to put things in better perspective and to retrieve more memories of the good times, which somehow I had managed to bury.

It's the kind of one-on-one conversation that many parents—maybe *all* parents—need to have with their grown-up children. But perhaps most of all it needs to be initiated by divorced parents who are separated from their children not only by miles but also by regrets.

Like so many other things in life, our regrets, when we confront them, may turn out to have less basis than we believe in our guilt-distorted, fear-exaggerated thoughts. But even if the regrets are real, even if our children tear at the pale flesh of our exposed vulnerability, at least we have confronted reality, and our children know where we stand. And that is progress—by anybody's yardstick.

A week after Grant left, he wrote and thanked me for the visit. A few months later Jay wrote. He was ready to come to Philadelphia to see me and Marilyn. He was apprehensive about it, he wrote, not as comfortable as he wished he could be, but he wanted to see us.

I arranged for his airplane ticket, and the night before he arrived, I told Marilyn:

"You know, I'm scared to death."

"You know, I am, too."

Chapter 13

Tradition: A Tie That Binds

Eastern Airlines flight 596 was due in from Charlotte at 1:16 in the afternoon, but by noon the television monitors at Philadelphia International Airport showed an indefinite delay. At 1:45 the announcement came that the flight had been canceled. The thought that flickered in my mind was: I hope this isn't prophetic.

What do you say to a son you haven't seen for almost four years? What do you think about as you stand, sit, stand, and pace nervously at the airport? I examined first my relationship with Grant. Why had we done so well so quickly? What had enabled us to rebuild from the ashes of that wretched day in the drugstore when he had turned away and told me that he didn't want to talk to me? How had we gone from that to the Algonquin Hotel, and the final healing that was produced?

What I now knew was that Grant and I had enjoyed far more satisfying, close times together than I had allowed myself to remember—perhaps because my guilt over leaving clouded my memory. There had been our times together on our bicycles, with our tabletop hockey game, at the baseball park, in the

226

yard with our zoysia grass pluggers, in front of the television set on football Sundays. We had a foundation on which to build anew our relationship. We had some tradition. To each other we could say, "Do you remember when we . . ."

And then I tried to replay my relationship with Jay. What troubled me was that we didn't have much tradition to fall back on. We lacked the mortar with which to stick together the bricks of our lives. Or did we? Was I falling into the same trap with Jay that I had with Grant? Was I forgetting the sweet and focusing solely on the sour? No, as I reflected, the blanching truth was that Jay and I really hadn't done so many things together. The wrestling, punching, and horsing around that I had done with Grant over the years never appealed much to Jay, who was more intellectual than physical.

The only roughhousing in which he participated with me and Grant was a game that I had made up when they were about six and seven and that involved, strangely enough, make-believe killer ants. A long time ago, I had seen a Charlton Heston movie titled *The Naked Jungle,* which featured, in addition to Heston, an army of ants that devoured everything in sight, including people. The term that the natives had for the ants sounded like "marabunta," and I never forgot it. It became part of my vocabulary, and anybody who seemed insensitive or overly aggressive became, to me, a "marabunta." One night on television Jay, Grant, and I happened to see *The Naked Jungle,* and, by golly, they went "marabunta" mad, too. I suggested a game in which we would sit on the floor and they would try to capture the "marabunta" that were represented by my running fingers, which darted over and under my folded legs and occasionally found their way into the stomachs and ribs of Jay and Grant. They absolutely loved the game and the entire "Bunta" family that we made up—Mary, Freddie, Charlie, and Herman. They always appeared in that sequence, and Herman was, in our language, "the baddest Bunta of all," and he was almost impossible for them to catch. Their catching amounted, usually, to Grant's grabbing my hand and holding it while Jay pounded on it with his fist.

Every night, it seemed, when I walked in the door, the first thing I heard were cries of "Bunta! Bunta!" and that meant that it was time to start the game. It was a delight, and it made coming home something to anticipate with a special eagerness.

But for the most part, especially as he became a teenager, Jay was quiet and nonphysical. In moments of turmoil he turned inward. When I screamed, he went to his room. He didn't scream back—as Grant sometimes did—and he seemed to carry around with him much of the unpleasantness that Grant somehow was able to get rid of.

Grant and I could clash, but fifteen minutes later he would be out in the driveway shooting baskets and challenging me to a game of 21 points. When Jay and I argued, the mending was more difficult because often neither of us seemed to know what to say or how to say it.

"Jay, I'm sorry for what I said, but, dammit, sometimes I'd like to wring your neck."

"Daddy, I'm sorry, too—but when you'd like to wring my neck, you really get mad at me, and I'm not comfortable with that."

"Sometimes I wish you weren't so sensitive."

"Sometimes I wish you were more sensitive."

"Oh, come on, Jay . . ."

"What do you mean—'come on'?"

At 4:15 in the afternoon a flight swished in, and my stomach told me that this was *the* flight, the one that would bring Jay to Philadelphia. I stood at the head of the ramp, my mouth dry, my palms wet, just as when Grant first came. What would he look like? People can change a lot in four years. He was a high school senior when I last saw him. Now he was a college senior, eight weeks away from graduation.

The passengers began to appear on the ramp, and mechanically I began to count them—as I always do when I'm at the airport to write a story. There's something essential that specificity brings to an account: "He was the 41st passenger through the door and . . ." My silent count mounted: 24, 25, 26 . . . 37, 38, 39 . . . Jay was the 63d passenger, a carefully groomed young man in a pale-blue oxford button-down shirt, bright-green V-neck sweater, and neat khaki pants. He looked so very much as old pictures from college showed that I looked at twenty-one. I grabbed his arm with enthusiasm and told him that I was glad to see him again. He managed a smile and said that with the airplane mix-up he wasn't certain he'd ever arrive, but "I finally made it . . . and it's good to be here."

In some ways he was like a stranger, like somebody

else's son who was graduating with a degree in psychology and then planning to go to a theological seminary in Oklahoma. When we talked, it was very much the same as when we exchanged letters: words came out, but not feelings. Yes, he was glad that school was almost finished; yes, he was looking forward to summer. Yes, I liked living and working in Philadelphia; yes, my book was on schedule, and I felt good about it.

From the very beginning Jay and Marilyn hit it off, and he told me, "I really like her." On the surface Jay and I hit it off too, but I felt that we were like two evenly matched boxers in the early rounds—tentatively going through the motions without taking any risks. I had promised myself that I would take it easy. I would keep the bridle in place and not say too much too quickly. After all, it had taken Grant and me three visits and hours of talking and listening to reach the point where we shared comfortably the things that we felt most deeply. I didn't want to push Jay. I would start slowly, and then, if it seemed appropriate—and only then—I gingerly would tiptoe into the fringes of what ultimately I knew we had to discuss: Why I had left, how I felt then and how I felt now about him and Grant, how sorry I was that my fathering hadn't been better.

The three of us went out to dinner, and it was almost eleven o'clock when we walked back to the condominium through a light rain that was whipped by wind that howled through the tunnels created by the tall buildings in Philadelphia's center city. No sooner had we reached our home in the sky on the thirty-seventh floor than the telephone summoned our attention.

I answered and immediately recognized the voice of a neighbor.

"I've been trying to reach you . . ."

"Yes?"

"We just had our first tragedy in the building. If you go out on your terrace and look down, you can see what I mean. The police are here, but I don't think too many people know about it yet."

"Thanks, Al. I'll take a look."

Out on the terrace, four hundred feet above street level, I squinted down into the dark courtyard, which opens off the fifth story and which is hidden from public view by the back wall of the ancient Academy of Music on the east and the horseshoe bend of the condominium on the other three sides. At first I saw nothing. The fountain was silent—as it always was so late in the evening.

But what was that—over there by the glass doors that connect the courtyard to the indoor swimming pool? It was a man—or rather the lifeless form of a man—sprawled face down on the pebbled concrete of the courtyard floor, arms and legs extended like a rag doll. The body was dressed in what looked like a tan leisure suit, and as the rain's intensity increased, the swimming pool doors opened and two men came outside and carefully tucked a clear plastic sheet around the body.

My eyes tracked up the side of the building, following the line on which the body must have fallen. Yes, there it was—an open window on the thirty-first floor. The wind sucked out the yellow curtains, which flapped furiously against the brick face of the building.

"Marilyn. Somebody has jumped and killed himself."

She came through the sliding door from the bedroom, looked down and whispered, "Oh, my God."

Through the coarse draperies that partially shielded the terrace from our living room, I saw Jay, already in his pajamas and reading on the sofa that converted to our guest bed.

"Jay," I called softly, as I slid open the door. "There's been an accident. A man is dead. He's down there now."

Jay slipped into his robe and studied the scene below. Four men were around the body now, and they seemed to be tracing its outline on the concrete. A flashbulb popped as one of them snapped a picture.

"Are they policemen?" Jay asked, his face pale and drawn. The last time I had seen him look like that was on the night of Grant's accident, when he had hugged my neck and told me how terrible it was.

"Yes, they're policemen."

"It's awful," Jay mumbled. "Why would anybody do it?"

"He must have thought he'd run out of reasons to live."

"It's awful," Jay repeated. "I'm not sure I'll be able to sleep now."

"Well, let's try; it's late."

All of us tried, but none of us had much success. My sleep was riddled by nightmares of my falling through space, screaming, flailing my arms and trying insanely to grab enough air to cushion myself against the concrete that rushed up to meet me.

The next morning I was up before the six thirty alarm, and the morning was bright and cheerful-looking with the prospect of a glorious sunrise suggested by streaks of orange in thin clouds that seemed to hang just beyond the Delaware River to the east. Down in the courtyard there was scant evidence of the death scene that had been played out the night before. A circle of dampness marked the spot, and off to the left a green hose was neatly curled in a pile, like a sleeping snake. The maintenance people already had been at work, and those in the building who arose now and looked down would have no inkling that anything had happened—at least not until they read the newspapers.

Inside, Jay was stirring in the kitchen, making coffee.

"Hi, did you get any sleep?" I asked.

"No, I really felt bad. I still do. I'm not sure I'll ever feel comfortable here."

* * * * *

While I had promised myself that I would go slowly in talking about the things that mattered with Jay, I found, as the visit neared its end, that I was pushing, almost desperately at times. Although I recognized what I was doing, I seemed powerless to stop. I had abandoned the game plan completely.

"Jay, I want very much for us to have a caring relationship—like I have with Grant."

"I couldn't ever feel that you were my father."

"That's all right. What kind of relationship do you think we could have?"

"We could be friends, I suppose, but probably not very close friends. I don't think we have too much in common."

His religion was the most important factor in his life, he said, and he felt that he couldn't share it with me because I wouldn't understand. I suggested that he try, because I might understand more than he thought. But he doubted that I would understand— ever.

"Jay, in the last few years I've made it a point to tell all the people who matter to me that they do matter. I said everything to Pop. I've told Mom. Marilyn knows. Grant knows. You're the only one I haven't told, and it's important for me to say this: You matter to me very much."

Jay squirmed on the kitchen countertop, where he sat as he and I munched peanut butter on crackers and sipped diet cola. "I'm not sure something like that needs to be said," he commented flatly. "I've always felt that what people do is more important than what they say."

The hair on my neck seemed to rise in anger. He was doing to my face what he had done to me by letter before. He wasn't going to let me off the hook. He was going to stick it in me and then twist it—until the pain was unbearable. Already it was hurting, but I forged on, mentally lashing myself for the strategic error I was committing but not able to divert myself from this course of action.

"Jay, I want to tell you the same thing I told Grant: I'm sorry about how I was as a father when you were growing up. I'm sorry for all the things I didn't do. I wish I could go back and try again, but I can't. The best I can do is tell you that I'm sorry."

He said that he had tried to put those times behind him, but "I haven't been able to forget." Could he forgive? He was trying, he said, but it wasn't easy. The pain seemed to seep all the way into the marrow of his bones, he said.

On the last day I asked him not to shut the door on the possibility of a caring relationship with me. Actually, I almost begged, and the expression in his eyes seemed to suggest: I didn't know it mattered so much to you. He told me that he hadn't intended to shut the door but that he wanted me to know where he stood, how he felt and how he might always feel. But he didn't want to hurt me, he said, because all of us already had gone through enough pain for our lifetimes.

I was easier to talk to, he said, than he had imagined I would be. I seemed mellow and gentle, and that had surprised him. "That's not the way I remember you." We walked through rain to a pet store so that he could show me a macaw like the one he hoped to own someday. On the way back to the condominium, he said, "I can't believe that you're willing to get out in the rain and go look at birds with me."

I was puzzled. "Why not? What's so unusual about that?"

"Don't you remember the last time I asked you to go to a pet shop with me?"

"No . . . when was that?"

"I must have been about twelve or fourteen, and we were in the mall and I said, 'Hey, let's look at those rabbits in the window,' and you said—"

"I'm not sure I want to know what I said."

"You said: 'Aw, come on. Let's don't waste our time with that. Why's a kid your age interested in rabbits anyway?' You don't remember, do you?"

"No, I don't . . . Jay, I'm sorry for what I was. Really sorry."

"I'm glad you're not that way now."

Jay told Marilyn that he had enjoyed his visit and that he would like to come again sometime. On the way to the airport he talked about what he would be doing the next day, when the theme park where he had worked for four summers would be holding a staff meeting.

At the airport we found that lightning had struck twice. His return flight had been canceled—because of an electrical malfunction in the jetliner—but he could get to Charlotte eventually by catching an Air Canada flight to Miami, if he hurried. The Miami-bound jet was ready to leave, and he and I ran toward the ramp. Our farewell was brief.

"I'm glad you came," I called.

"Me too. I got to run. Bye."

He disappeared through the door, and I walked slowly toward the airport parking garage. I felt disappointed, flat and miserable, and I was trying to figure out why. Realistically, the visit had gone as well as I could have expected. But the problem was that it had not gone as well as I unrealistically had hoped. I had wanted everything, but I had gotten only a piece of it. The scar tissue still was there, and I had to come to grips with the reality that it might always be there. Perhaps he and I never would be any closer. Maybe I

was lucky to have this much. After all, some fathers
. . .

I tried to put it out of my mind, but I couldn't.

* * * * *

In the months that followed Jay's visit, business
took me to North Carolina three times, and as Jay
and I continued to grope to become reacquainted, I
sensed that his feelings toward me were softening.
One night after dinner, when Grant had left us to
return to his campus apartment, Jay turned down the
car radio and began to talk to me—carefully, almost
as if he had rehearsed a presentation. He told me that
he was proud of the person I had become. I was not
so intolerant; I didn't holler; I didn't seem to get
angry, he said. My old priorities of work, myself, and
golf no longer seemed to burden my soul. I seemed
happy and gentle. Marilyn, he said, must have been a
very good influence on me.

"Thanks, Jay."

"We can be friends. I want very much for us to be
friends."

A year slipped past, and Jay announced that he
would like to come to Philadelphia again for a visit.
He arrived, and right from the start things were
markedly different from the first time. His airplane
landed two minutes ahead of schedule, and nobody
jumped out of the condominium. By week's end both
of us sensed that we were on our way toward
reestablishing a relationship—not as good as we had
once had, but far better than the last few years. It had
taken so much time, energy, and patience, but now it
was paying off for both of us. I prayerfully thanked

the friends I once had cursed—the friends who had beseeched me to "give him time; give him time."

Jay was an up-front young man with a sense of who he was and what he wanted out of life, and while he cautiously kept track of every penny in his bank account, he was not hesitant to spend money on things he wanted. From summer and weekend jobs over the years he had saved enough to pay cash for a new Mazda, treat himself to a $650 wristwatch, and splurge on a drawerful of $29 Polo shirts in an eye-opening assortment of colors that ranged from purple to orange.

One rainy afternoon—it always seemed to rain when Jay was in Philadelphia—the two of us sat and talked for hours, not as father and son but as two friends. Yes, he said, he no longer felt that there was anything about which we couldn't and shouldn't talk—if we wanted to.

What, I asked him, had it been like in the very beginning after I had moved away from him, Grant, and their mother?

"I felt like I was an outcast. At that point I didn't know many kids with divorced parents. I lied a lot to cover it up. People would call and ask for you, and I'd say that you weren't home but that you'd be back later. It just didn't seem appropriate to say that you weren't with us anymore. I felt kind of like it was my fault. I felt that maybe I was too religious and that it had driven you out of the house. Grant probably was more hurt than I was, but he never talked about it."

Jay got up from the sofa, walked to the terrace, and then returned. It seemed difficult for him to continue, yet he obviously wanted to talk.

"You left," he said, "and I took it as a personal rejection. I thought that if you loved me so much, how could you leave? Time has altered my feelings about this, for the most part. But back then I felt that if you didn't care about me, I wouldn't care about you either. My feeling was that anybody could be a biological father, but if you were a real father, how could you do this to us?"

In that crunch, Jay said, children have no choice but to choose up sides. "There's an immediate need to align yourself with one parent. It's hard not to. You have to survive, and for survival you have to side with the other parent, the one who didn't leave. If you don't, then you feel that maybe you'll be rejected by that parent too—and then you'll have nobody."

What about the letter, Jay—the "Dear Darrell" letter that demanded that I get out of your life?

"Back then I hated myself and everybody else. It wasn't hard for me to hate you—I was shy and didn't have many friends. Finally, God gave me a better self-image, and I started to like myself. Then he helped me to like others and then to love others. Today I feel incapable of hating anybody. 'Hate' no longer is in my vocabulary."

Jay said that he couldn't think of anybody he didn't like now. He studied me and smiled faintly. "If the same thing happened again, if we were together and then you left, I don't think I'd react the same way. No, I'm sure I wouldn't. I have changed a lot since those days—and you have too."

I had wanted to share with Jay, but I was getting even more than I had bargained for. He was laying it all out for me—candidly, unflinchingly, but not without some discomfort.

A major force in overcoming his negative feelings about himself, Jay said, was a book titled *Making Contact.* "The thing I remember most from the book was that it said that the farther down within a person you go, the more alike people are. People have the same basic needs, share the same basic feelings. Before that, I'd always felt so alone."

Since leaving college a year ago, Jay had walked away from the path that successful people are supposed to follow. He worked as a retail clerk and as a waiter in the months when the theme park was closed.

"People look at what I do and think I'm wasting time. I'm not successful by their definition of success—making money and having a responsible position. But I've learned a lot—I *am* learning a lot—as far as reaching out to people, knowing myself, learning how to take chances. I'm learning how to live instead of just going through life."

When he goes into the ministry, as he eventually will, he said, he'll be better prepared because he'll know a little more about how the world turns. No, he said, he didn't regret the early years in upper-middle-class affluence in the suburbs. "I'd be a lot worse off if I had been poor . . . The American dream is not really so great. Affluence can't support happiness. I know it—and I don't have to spend my whole life working toward it and then be disappointed. Now I feel good that I can enjoy things like a new car and a new watch, but they don't have hold of me; I have hold of them. They don't use me; I use them. I'm out of step with many people my age. I'm not less materialistic necessarily, but our values are different. I got into self-growth before I got into making money."

Suddenly I felt in awe of my son, who was sharing his truths as he saw them—in a way that some people never are able to, out of fear that others will think less of them or even reject them. Jay seemed not to be concerned about that, and I wanted to tell myself that it was because he felt secure enough with me now that he knew that rejection was not a possibility.

In a way, he said, it probably was a good thing that I had left and broken up the family. "I'd not be the person I am if you had stayed. I wouldn't have been free to be what I have become. If you'd stayed, you would have sat on me about what you always considered my overinvolvement in religion."

He didn't invite me to respond, but I did anyway. I was happy, I said, that his religion had helped him turn outward and consider the essential nature of relationships with other people. Long ago, I said, I had feared that his religion was causing him to shut others from his life, out of the feeling that others, if they weren't as religious, weren't good enough to be his friends. Yes, I told him, I was convinced that he probably was right, that my staying would have had an inhibiting effect on his development. I told him that I also was convinced that our relationship was going to prosper despite the many differences in our philosophies of life. Differences didn't have to divide—not if people were able to respect without reservation each other's individuality. "We can do that, Jay. I know we can do that."

"Yes," he answered. "I'm sure that we can do that."

I wanted to hug him, but I didn't. What I did do was tell him, "You're a remarkable young man."

"It's good to hear that from you. For so many years I thought that you considered me anything but remarkable."

* * * * *

I never knew before how important tradition is in binding relationships securely against hard times. Now I know. Grant and I could sit and talk and I could say: "Grant, do you remember the time when you needed three strikeouts in your last Little League game to have 50 for the season? You struck out two in the first inning and then in the second inning you struck out the first batter, and you looked over at me in the stands and waved."

"Yeah, I'll never forget that."

Because Jay and I had so little tradition to fall back on, we had to start almost from scratch and build *new* tradition. We've had an elegant lunch at the elegant Hotel Hershey, which stands atop a hill within sight of the smokestacks that rise from the chocolate factory. We've gone to Hershey Park, down in the valley, and ridden and re-ridden the incredible roller coaster that turns a complete loop. We've gaped at the floral beauty of Longwood Gardens, on the road to Baltimore. We've gone to a Moroccan restaurant, sat on the floor and eaten with our fingers. We've watched *A Chorus Line* and discussed the profanity, sexual overtones, and the foot-stomping tunes. We've hummed together through *One Mo' Time* and then bought the original-cast album—so that when we play it, we can relive that memorable evening at the Shubert Theatre.

We're getting there—because we're trying. But because so much of what has happened has caused me to focus on building tradition, I've begun to question friends about the traditions they cherish with their children.

One man who was quick to share with me was Philadelphia lawyer Gilbert M. Cantor, who once had taken a cross-country motorcycle trip with his two sons—more than 3,000 miles in 12 days. What a tradition builder that must have been.

Yes, it surely was, said Cantor, and as his face glowed with warmth, I was certain that he was reliving and savoring all over again that magnificent event in his life ten years ago, when David was seventeen and Paul was almost sixteen—not yet old enough to drive his own bike, so he piggybacked with his father. The journey took them from Philadelphia through the mountains and deserts to Los Angeles. Then they shipped the bikes back by air freight.

"It was a great experience for family development," Cantor said. "It turned out to be even more important and valuable than I knew when we did it. We always talked about it—and we still do. One of them will say, 'Do you remember when Dad's bike fell over?' and then we'll laugh about that all over again."

Cantor began to reminisce. "I'd had a bike a couple of years, and I'd sit with the boys and talk about it. We'd taken some short trips after David was old enough to have his own bikes. One day one of them said: 'Wouldn't it be nice if we headed out and just kept going?' Yes, we agreed, how about if we went to California? We talked about the trip for a long time.

243

It was just great. We planned what we'd need, and we read accounts of other people's trips. We planned whether we'd camp out or sleep in. It really was a comical caravan. David wouldn't go without his guitar, and there it was—sticking up in the air from his bike."

Cantor said that they carried three sleeping bags and two tents. "It took us an hour to pack before we took off every morning. We went into the desert with plenty of water and food, and we had no bad weather. The mountains were more hazardous than the desert. Coming down some of the mountains, we felt as if we were coming almost straight down. It was wonderful."

Cantor said that he and his sons—one now lives in Washington, D.C., and the other in California—"have been closer since the trip than we ever had been. I committed 12 days to those boys in a way that you don't always do on normal vacations. I made a promise and carried it out—despite a certain amount of resistance elsewhere in the family."

Today Cantor is divorced—and remarried.

* * * * *

It was way back in 1962, and for Jack Katz, the six-year-old son of Philadelphia lawyer Leon Katz, it was time to join Indian Guides, the program in which father and son put on their feathered headbands, beat the tom-tom, and, most important of all, carve a block that becomes part of their tribe's totem pole at the end-of-the-year camp meeting.

Katz, who today is a judge in Philadelphia's Court of Common Pleas, and formerly was a chancellor of the Philadelphia Bar Association, said that the totem

244

pole block posed what seemed to be an insurmount-
able obstacle for him. "I am devoid of mechanical
aptitude, and it's difficult for me to build anything.
But what could I do? This was important to Jack. We
couldn't have the worst-looking block in the whole
tribe. So I bought a set of carving tools, and we
worked together, the way father and son work together at that age, when there's a closeness that's
never again repeated. We carved a block with a face
like Clutch Cargo, the cartoon character, the guy with
the stone face, with the square jaw. We painted it
blue and green. At camp we put our block on the
totem pole, and I think I was prouder of it than Jack.
It was the first thing I ever made . . . and for years we
talked about it. It was *our* block."

The years passed and by 1978 Jack Katz was
twenty-two and a first-year law student. His sister was
twenty-four and lived in her own apartment. Katz and
his wife, Irene, now lived alone in their four-bed-
room home in the suburbs, where they had lived
since the children were tiny. It was too much house
for them now, so they bought a unit in a condominium right smack in the middle of Philadelphia. But
they couldn't take everything with them, they agreed,
and they began the process of deciding what to leave
behind.

What would they do with all the mementos from
their children's growing-up years—the letters written
during summer camps, the model airplanes, the auto-
graphed baseballs, the glove and bats . . . and the
totem pole block from Indian Guides?

Katz said that he and his wife "offered these things
to the children, but they didn't share our emotional-

ism about them. I asked Jack about the airplane models and the totem pole block and he said, 'Just throw them away.' He took furniture and things that he could use in his apartment, but he took nothing to which we had attached our memories."

They decided to have a garage sale, and Katz "was too chicken to attend. I was spared the trauma of watching our memories being gobbled up." The next day, a rainy Sunday, Katz and his wife cleaned their house of what was left over from the sale. Among the leftovers was the totem pole block, some of the books from which they had read bedtime stories to their children, records, and models . . . and memories of times forever gone.

They loaded their memories into trash bags and carried them one at a time through the rain and placed them next to the curb, the burial of twenty years. "We were drenched with sadness and water. Each trip to the curb was like a funeral procession without music. I wondered if it was too late to turn back, to stop, to reclaim our memories and our house and a part of our lives that meant so much to us. But it was too late. The house was sold, empty of children and furniture."

As they filled the bags, they said nothing, each silent in thought. Katz excused himself as they came down to the final bag and told his wife he was going upstairs to see if they'd left anything behind. "I knew damned well we hadn't left anything, but I had to go back one last time. I walked through the bedrooms, and I almost could hear the children's laughter, their cries, their screams."

Then he came back downstairs, red-eyed, and put

the totem pole block into the last trash bag. "It was like putting part of myself into the bag . . . but I had nowhere to keep it."

Together Leon and Irene Katz carried that bag through the drizzle, and then she went back into the house, fetched a plastic cover, and stretched it over all the bags—to keep the memories safe and dry until tomorrow's trash pickup. It was, Katz said, a ritual not unlike tucking the children into bed.

They got into their car and drove away. Katz never looked back, but he thought: What have we done?

* * * * *

Jay, Grant, and I never had taken a 3,000-mile motorcycle trip, but we had created our own totem pole block—when we were in Indian Guides in Louisville. We were part of the Algonquin tribe—I had thought about the irony of that as my love affair developed with the Algonquin Hotel—and our assignment was to create a block with the letter *G* . . . to help spell out Algonquin.

Like Leon Katz, I had no woodworking ability either, and I had huffed, puffed, and argued with Jay and Grant during construction.

"That is a funny-looking *G*," Grant said.

"You think you could do better?"

"No, but it's funny-looking. Everybody will laugh at it."

"How about if you stop talking and start painting?"

Jay had wanted to paint the block red and blue. Grant had wanted some green on it. I didn't care. I just wanted to get it finished.

"Daddy," Jay said, "red, blue, and green will look silly."

"You and your brother want to fight each other to decide the colors?"

"Oh, Daddy . . ."

We painted it red, blue, and green, and it did look silly. And the *G* was funny-looking. But when we took it to the tribe meeting, nobody laughed—because everybody else's looked just as funny. For a while we cherished the block, but in the move from Louisville we lost it.

I always regretted that.

Chapter 14

The Future . . .
and the Pitfalls

The letter was from Jay—the kind of letter that every parent hopes to receive from a child but that few of us ever do. What made the letter remarkable was twofold:

—It described the mind-boggling changes that have taken place in Jay in the years since he and I lived together as father and son. When I knew him then, he was a quiet child who tried to blend into the wallpaper when he was in a crowd and who was so attuned to the possibility of failure that he was hesitant to undertake again anything that he hadn't previously completed—and could complete again—with success. Now, by his own account, he had become freewheeling, and he was savoring every drop of his new life.

—It spoke in a low-key way of how far our relationship—his and mine—has come since the shadowy years when we groped for each other but couldn't connect.

Here is the letter:

"Sunday night 16 of us got off work at the theme park at 6 o'clock and left for the Chattooga River near Clayton, Ga. We got to the Black Mountain

State Park about 10:30, and then we cooked out at our campsites. Since we were short of tents, some of us, including me, slept in sleeping bags under the stars. It was the first time that I had ever gone camping, although it was something that I'd wanted to do for a long time.

"In the early morning it got very windy and foggy, and I got cold. We got up, went into Clayton and ate breakfast at the Heart of Rabun motel, and then we went to the river. We had five rafts with our group, four to a raft plus a guide. We got on the river around 11 o'clock. The scenery was unbelievable. We ate lunch on some big rocks and made lemonade with spring water from a waterfall. I fell out of the raft once, and fell once while climbing a rock. I'm a little sore, but it's nothing serious. We stopped in Seneca, S.C., which is near Clemson, at a steak house for dinner. We had a waitress who was one of those rare, special people in the world. One of us finally asked why she was so happy, and she said: 'Why not? I have a wonderful husband and fantastic children.' She kept coming back and talking to us.

"We went through a lot of small towns like Fair Play, S.C., and finally got on the interstate and home around 11 p.m. It was great! You should try white-water rafting sometime. You'd love it.

"I've accepted a job as a waiter at a restaurant that has a menu that is 18 pages long, including the wine list. After I get settled into my routine I'm going to inquire about taking some banjo lessons. I enjoy banjo music and if it isn't too expensive, I might just learn how to play it. I've been saying for several years that there are three things I really want to do someday: fly an airplane, scuba dive, and play the banjo.

"I've been learning a lot lately about making decisions, presenting myself, and meeting people. I'm also beginning to learn how to really live. That was one of my goals to reach before I go away to school. Learning how to remove fear was a big part of that. Most people don't do new things because they're bound by fear.

"The trip to Georgia was with two foremen from the theme park, and on the way back—late at night—I talked a lot about serious things, which is what I do when I'm tired. I surprised myself at how much I talked about you. It seems like the more we get to know each other, as each of us is now, the more I miss seeing you. When are you coming to Charlotte?"

* * * * *

Marilyn and I had flown into St. Louis, where we met Grant, who came up from Charlotte, and then the three of us rented a car and drove 120 miles to Jefferson City to spend a week with my mother, whose accommodation to widowhood had exceeded everybody's expectations, including, I believe, her own.

It was late on one of those muggy Missouri afternoons, when the western sky was smeared with orange and purple and the empty promise of rain, and Grant and I sat on folding lawn chairs in the backyard, near the grill, with beers in hand and mellowness in mind.

"Grant, what about that day at the drugstore—the day after I had left home, when you walked away and wouldn't talk? I don't think I ever hurt more in my life. What was going on inside you that day?"

"I was confused. I didn't understand."

"What changed things?"

"Now I understand—as much as it's possible for somebody else to understand—and I accept what happened."

Meeting Marilyn and recognizing the quality of her character had been a big factor in helping him—and Jay too, he thought—understand that I didn't have fangs and that I hadn't grown horns because I had moved away from them and their mother. No, Grant said, anybody who could hook up with somebody like Marilyn had to be better than all right. It wouldn't be stretching the point, he said, to suggest that Marilyn was the best thing that ever happened to me.

I wanted to know how Grant felt about the break-up of the marriage. Had it changed his views about his ever getting married? When somebody so young is exposed at short range to so much pain, is it fear-inspiring?

Grant put down his beer and poked around in the charcoal under the pork chops on the grill. "It scared me . . . and for a while I said that I'd never get married, that I'd never put myself in a position where that could happen to me, where I'd cause myself and so many others to suffer so much. But I've changed my mind about that. Nothing is guaranteed in life, and if you're not willing to take a chance, you're not going to get much out of life."

No, Grant said, he had nothing against marriage—to the right woman—but he was certain that he wouldn't want marriage until he was older, perhaps close to thirty, when his career in accounting was established and when he had done the things that single, foot-free people have the luxury of doing.

"You really think you'll wait until you're thirty?" I asked.

He grinned. "I can say it now, but if the right person came along, I might be tempted to change my mind. If that happens, remind me of what I said today, will you?"

"Would you listen to me?"

"Probably not. But tell me anyway."

We turned the pork chops as the sky darkened and thunder rumbled far, far away. "You want another beer?" I asked.

"No; I want to talk to you."

"What about?"

"About my future . . . You know, always before, kids have been able to grow up with the realistic expectation that they could surpass their parents' standard of living, that they could earn more money, have a nicer house, take longer trips, advance farther in their careers. That's always how it's been, but it's not like that anymore."

I asked him what he meant.

"With the economy like it is, there's no hope for me ever to have it as good again as I had it when I was growing up, in the suburbs, with you and Mom. It's just not possible—a mustard-colored house, a station wagon and sports car . . . the things that represent some kind of security and success. You know what I mean?"

Yes, I told Grant, I knew what he meant.

"Here I am in my twenties, and I've already had it

better than I'm ever going to have it again. That's really crazy, isn't it?"

"Are you sorry that you had it good when you were growing up?"

No, Grant said, he didn't regret a minute of it—because he had tasted what it was like to live in the upper-middle-class world. "I'll tell you something: It taught me that money and success don't necessarily make people happy. That'll make it easier for me, I suppose, to scale down my expectations about what I want out of life. I do want to be happy. Above all else, I want to be happy."

I told Grant that with that outlook, his priorities seemed in order.

"I've always felt that I was loved by you and Mom—even after you left and things got so bad. I'm fortunate, because I have a good self-image. You don't have to worry about me. I may complain, but I'll be OK."

* * * * *

I feel good about Jay and Grant and their ability to rise above the muck and mire into which they were dragged by the separation and divorce. But not infrequently I wonder if the hard times left scars that not yet have surfaced, scars that in the years to come could alter the course of their lives and allow them less than the full bite for which they are striving and to which, I believe, they are entitled.

It's a question that I have discussed on more than one occasion with therapists who daily confront the wreckage that inevitably follows the breaking of families. One of those who spoke to the issue was

254

psychologist Herbert G. Zerof, who is director of the Marriage and Family Institute in Charlotte and who was the counselor to whom my former wife and I turned in the waning years of our marriage.

What did Zerof think about the impact of divorce on children? This is the picture that he drew:

By their attitudes and by their behavior, divorcing parents determine to a large extent how their children will be affected. If parents successfully turn loose of each other and build new lives, they tend to enable their children to escape the divorce trauma with minimal damage. But if parents hang on desperately and try to live with what used to be rather than with what is, they sow the seeds of disillusionment, distrust, and disgust in their children's lives.

A key element in how children handle their parents' divorce is how the parents themselves handle it. If one of the parents blames the other, if one is right and the other is wrong, it's easy for the children to be influenced. This is particularly true if there is a solid peg on which to hang blame—if the father has run off with another woman or if the mother has moved in with another man. In one of the worst cases that he ever saw, Zerof said, a "woman who was vitriolic beyond belief never could forgive the husband for leaving. One time she took the kids—they were seven and nine—to the other lady's house, knocked on the door and told them, 'Now you're going to see the slut that your Daddy's been staying with.'

"Sometimes I see this happening, this kind of hanging on, even after four or six years, and the kids are flunking in school, not sleeping right, not feeling good. It's incredible how long it can go on"—and the impact that it can have on the helpless and hapless children.

For the sake of the children, divorcing parents have to make some resolution about cutting each other out of their lives. The people who seem able to turn loose with the least difficulty are those who want to get on with living, who have other things in their lives. They tend not to remain so enmeshed with the other person because they have something else to go to—another person, a career, a new life-style. But if a vacuum exists, it's a different story. Some people let the world cave in on them and they stop seeing friends. The person who has been left feels rejected, and it's more difficult to turn loose. The person with a healthy self-image always seems to do best, but it's always painful. It's not possible to overemphasize that: It's always painful.

How long does it take reasonably healthy people to move each other from the center stage of their lives?

Probably at least a year, and it's a mistake to try to force it, because a reasonable period of mourning must take place after a marriage dies—just as mourning must follow the death of a loved one. If mourning is cut short, the feelings that were suppressed invariably resurface at some later time, perhaps in disguise.

Divorced parents further can minimize the impact on children if they will stay in their parenting roles—because this has the effect of keeping children in their proper role, as children. Not infrequently therapists see some parents who become children and children who become parents to them. A father goes to pick up his children on the weekend, but they're busy. They'd rather stay where they are. So the father feels rejected, shows it and acts more like a child than a parent. He doesn't realize that the children have their own lives and that they are now occupied.

How much should children be told about the reasons behind the divorce?

His opinion, Zerof said, is that total truth generally is the best policy. Secrets are bad for all family members, including children. If one parent is running around, this will emerge eventually—whether the children are told right away or not.

If one parent is insane in some way and the other wants a divorce, the children should know. It may cause heartbreak now, but the trauma would be substantially greater if they found out five years later.

It's a fact that many children, like Grant, secretly think that their divorcing parents will get back together and that the family will be united and happy again. Should this misconception—if that's what it is—be confronted and punctured by the parents?

No, not usually, Zerof said. For the children this is not unlike believing in Santa Claus, and they gradually grow out of it. Parents probably don't need to dispel the notion. Unless the children inordinately stress it, there's no reason for parents actively to destroy the dream. Often when it is inordinately stressed, it's because one parent wants the same thing, that parent and the children feed each other . . . and that's not good.

Is *permanent* damage likely to result for the children when their parents divorce?

No, not really. While there tend to be far more repercussions from divorce than anybody imagined, the notion that this often causes permanent damage in children is not necessarily accurate. It's difficult to define what is meant by *permanent* damage. Some children from divorced families swear they'll never get divorced—no matter what—and this puts great pressure on the marriage to succeed, and they can't ever relax and enjoy the marriage. But mostly, therapists see children who, as adults, lead reasonable lives, who have friends and their share of good times.

* * * * *

One of the most treacherous pitfalls awaiting any divorcing parent is overvaluing the children—treacherous because it is cloaked in what seems to be a proper motive: giving the children the best that's possible.

Psychiatrist G. Pirooz Sholevar, director of child, adolescent, and family psychiatry at Thomas Jefferson University Medical College, said that overvalued children are in trouble—and so are their parents. "You can't talk about an overvalued child without talking about an undervalued parent," he said.

It's not difficult to identify those who are overvalued and undervalued. The mother wears what looks like a hand-me-down dress from her mother, while the daughter wears designer clothes. The father who never takes a vacation finances his daughter's trip to Europe, where she lives lavishly. A parent sends the child to the finest medical facilities in the country while the parent stands in line at a public clinic.

Overvalued children come in two varieties. On the one hand there is the child who was valued before divorce but later a parent makes a tremendous increase in the emotional investment in the child. On the other hand there is the child who was semi-ignored until the divorce, and then one parent who never had displayed much interest suddenly shows a surge of interest.

What happens to children who have been overvalued? Not uncommonly, their total development is distorted because they lack a realistic sense of themselves. Part of them feels as if they should be treated like nobility forever because they've been accustomed to getting everything they ask for. But the flip side is that they lack a basic sense of self-confidence and, as a result, they feel rotten about themselves.

We get our sense of self from trying things and finding out what we can do. But overvalued children don't try. They don't have to try—because everything is given to them. Most of us learn that we must earn what we get, that there are no handouts. But overvalued children don't learn this. The result is children who want everything but who feel that they don't deserve anything. It's the worst possible combination. The less these children feel they deserve, the more they ask for and the more they feel that they're not getting the right things.

One result is obvious: Unhappy, confused children who likely will develop into unhappy, confused adults.

Another possible result: These children forever feel indebted to the parent who overvalued them and feel obligated to pay back the parent—even at the expense of their own life. Therapists often see this in people who are in their fifties and sixties and whose parents are in their seventies and eighties. They try to pay back their parents by devoting their lives to them, and they miss their own opportunities. Some don't develop marital relationships. Others don't invest in careers. They remain with their parents to try to repay them.

It's not uncommon for divorced parents to deal with children in a perverse way that has the effect of forcing the children to grow up before their time and depriving them of childhood. Here is one example of how that can happen:

A significant number of divorced people become depressed—or more depressed. Some withdraw; some attempt suicide. Depressed parents don't dare go outside. So they stay home and invest in the child, and the result can be that the child becomes the caretaker of the parent. There is a flip-flop of roles and we have what therapists call "the parental child"—a reversal of generational lines. The child becomes the parent.

After most divorces there is a tendency by both parents to treat the child as a near-equal partner— regardless of the child's age. Frequently a therapist encounters a mother who asks her daughter: "How does my hair look? What about my clothes? Do you like my lipstick? Is this gown cut too low?" It may be too heavy to ask a ten-year-old girl these kinds of questions—but the questions often are asked because there no longer is a husband around to ask.

Divorced men are every bit as guilty as divorced women of this equalization of status. A not-uncommon trap into which middle-aged men tumble is treating a daughter in almost the same way they treat a girl friend who is not much older than the daughter. What happens is that the daughter feels that she no longer has a father figure.

Why do divorced parents behave this way? On the one hand it can be caused by crushing loneliness and the feeling that the child "is all I have." In this situation the demise of the parent-child relationship is almost inevitable—as is its replacement with a peer type of relationship. On the other hand parents may feel that a buddy relationship is easier for them to sustain with children whom they see infrequently. In the words of one father: "If I'm going to be with Tommy only one day a week, I don't want to have to behave like a father. I want us to have fun."

But the problem is this: Children don't want parents as friends; they want parents as parents. They're confused when the father suddenly becomes a big brother or the mother a big sister.

How can a divorced parent tell if he or she is overvaluing this child? Here are three questions that need to be considered:

What are the needs of the parent?
What are the needs of the child?
To what extent are the needs of both being satisfied?

If there is an imbalance in satisfying needs, it's obvious that a problem is building. If the bulk of energy and financial resources goes to satisfying the child and if there is little left for the parent, then the handwriting is on the wall. Clearly, everybody loses.

How can parents get out of the rut of overvaluing their children—once they acknowledge that they've fallen into the trap?

In therapy it's not unusual for divorced parents eventually to express a fantasy wish that they had no children so that their future chances for marriage and happiness won't be jeopardized. A question that often is asked is: "Who would want to marry somebody with three children?" It's a fantasy, to be sure, and generally parents don't bring it up until therapists coax it out of them. But then, with what they perceive as the therapist's permission, parents may acknowledge that, yes, their children are a burden.

This can cause heart-heavy feelings of guilt and in some instances it can lead to even greater overvaluation of children to try to compensate for the guilt. But it's the wise parent who realizes that guilt feelings are not abnormal in this situation, that many parents have them, and that the parent isn't a bad person for having them. Open acknowledgment of the burdensome aspects of parenting is critical because it helps give the parent a realistic basis for deciding to jump off the merry-go-round of overvaluing the child. It's amazing then how often the child picks up the parent's attitude change and quickly adopts new behavior. The result: A problem child not infrequently ceases to be such a problem upon recognizing that he or she no longer can get away with it.

This is the point at which everybody begins to win.

* * * * *

Over the years I've discussed the breakup of families not only with Jay and Grant but also with numbers of other children, many of whom were much younger than Jay and Grant. One of them, an eleven-year-old girl whose parents had separated, offered this advice for parents on how to explain separation to their children.

"When I first heard the news, I cried a little. So I advise parents to break it to the children easily, like saying: 'You know that we love each other and you too, but this is the best thing for us to do now. You will still see your father (or mother) but just not every day like you used to. And don't take it too hard, because it isn't as bad as all that.' "

Her advice to children: "Sometimes it isn't good for your parents to get a separation, but you must understand that the decision is up to them. Think about your parents' feelings. How are they going to feel? Try to talk to your parents about it. Ask them if maybe they should see a therapist. Maybe that could help. Remember that it is not only their duty to comfort you but your duty to comfort them, too."

If we listen to what our children are saying, we may get some insight not only into parenting but also into marriage—and how to keep it from ending in separation and divorce. What the children are telling us, it seems to me, can be distilled to this:

—Let us know you think that we're important. It's not just enough to be with us physically; we want you to be with us emotionally too.

—We like to see the two of you together, not just when you're with us but when you're not involved with us, just the two of you. It makes us feel good when you talk, laugh, love, share, and touch each other.

—We want you to let us know what the score is, what's going on with the two of you. If you keep us in the dark, if all we hear are yells but never explanations, we'll start to believe that whatever is wrong is our fault.

—We want you to stay together, but we also want you to be happy. If you can't stay together and be happy, then maybe it's best to live apart—at least for a while. At first it will be difficult for us, but we'll manage—if you'll help us. We know that divorce doesn't have to be the end of the world for you or for us, because so many of our friends' parents are divorced, and many of them are doing all right.

Yes, out of the mouths of babes can come words of wisdom—if we, as parents, ask and listen.

Are we asking? Are we listening?

It's my hope that we are. Good luck to all of us.

Epilogue

Not long ago, in a speech in the Philadelphia suburb of Wallingford, I talked about how I had struggled in the years after my divorce to tell my sons that I was sorry for the many times I had come up short as a father during their growing-up years. I asked them to forgive me for the needless shouting, for the inconsistencies in enforcing discipline, for the hundreds of weekends that I played golf and worked when I could have shared time with them.

It's the kind of conversation, I said, that every parent—especially every divorced parent—probably needs to have with every child, not only for the parent's sake but also for the child's.

A few days later I received a letter from a man who had been in the audience, and he agreed that many parents had fouled relationships with their children. But he also raised these questions: Aren't there just as many children who have done things for which they're sorry? Aren't there just as many children who, when they become adults, have the same reasons to say they're sorry?

Wouldn't it be wonderful, he wrote, if children somehow could gain earlier in life the appreciation for their parents that many of them seem to achieve later in life?

Yes, it would, I thought, but is it possible? Especially is it possible when children have faced the added dimension of divorce? It's traumatic enough when children mature, break the ties and leave home. But what about when a parent, by divorce, leaves home? How does a child deal with that?

I took my questions to psychiatrist Levon D. Tashjian, the father of three children, who works extensively with college students through his affiliation with Horsham Hospital near Ambler, Pennsylvania. Can parents, married or divorced, somehow create an atmosphere in which their children can appreciate and accept them now instead of perhaps later?

Yes, said Tashjian, it's possible, but the rub is that children tend to be caught between two forces that seem opposed to each other. One is that it's necessary for children to "devaluate" their parents as part of the process of leaving home or defending themselves against the pain of a parent's leaving. But the other force is forgiveness. If children don't forgive and make some peace with their parents, they tend not to be able to make peace with themselves.

Because the child has to devaluate the parents, for one reason or the other, there undoubtedly is truth in the old statement that the honest measure of a parent probably is somewhere between what the child thinks at eight and at eighteen. Part of this devaluation, even if the parents stay together, is prompted by pernicious societal influences. Children tend to feel cheated, and they focus on what they didn't get instead of on what they did get.

But even in the midst of devaluation, children often make some peace with their parents. They still may think that their parents are stupid, but the stupidity becomes less important and more tolerated. They don't need to fight their parents as they did before—and this, in fact, is partial forgiveness. A child may write or telephone a divorced parent and say nothing more than "Hi, how are you?" but this, in fact, may be partial forgiveness, too.

Part of children's appreciation for their parents comes through normal maturing. We can't see at twenty what we can see at forty. At twenty we're more at the center of our own universe. There is a sense of entitlement, of what one is owed—anything from material belongings to parents who are together, not divorced. There is heightened sense of self, and others are devalued. In others we tend to see the flaws instead of the good things. It's like listening to a record and hearing the scratches but not the music. The truth is that, yes, there are scratches and flaws, but there is also music.

How can a child be jarred from this heightened self-consciousness?

There is something to be said for work, for the donation of time, the philosophy of being able to invest in altruistic ways in something outside one's self. It is important for parents to help their children learn early about giving instead of always receiving. If we, as parents, indulge them excessively, give too much, try to make life too easy for them, we get spoiled children.

Why would parents do this? If parents are divorced, one obvious answer is that they want to make up for what they perceive that they have done to their children. They feel guilty, and they want their children to absolve them of their guilt. One way in which they may feel that they can encourage this absolution is to be too nice to their children. Experience tells us that this never works. Children are harmed—and so are parents.

There is another reason for spoiling children—a reason that may be less conscious than the other. It may be the result of parents who set out to prove that they are better parents than their own parents. In effect they revenge themselves on their parents. And what do they and those of us like them get for this? Part of our making peace with our own parents is seeing our children attack us as we attacked our parents. This is when we can say to our parents: "Hey, now I understand what you meant."

There is enlightened self-interest in not hating our parents. If we hate, we can expect our own children to have the same attitude toward us. There is no reason to think that we will be of more value to our children than our parents are to us. To think otherwise is part of our arrogance that comes back to haunt us.

It is critically important for parents, married and divorced, to begin setting the stage for forgiveness early with their children. We can't start at eighteen and say, "OK, it's time to forgive." This begins when we walk a fine balance between being authoritarian, providing necessary structure and firmness, and maintaining a certain elasticity, so that when we mess up, we can acknowledge it and apologize for it.

We can set a model for children with our own intimacy with our spouses, whether they are the children's parents or stepparents. We need to show our children the kind of intimacy that encourages sharing not only words but also feelings. Lack of an intimacy model can be crippling and can set the stage for our children to spend a lifetime wanting to get even with us for what we didn't give them.

Revenge is about the most stifling emotion that anybody can have. When your children need to get you for what you've done to them, they well may get you, but in the process they also will get themselves.

If, as divorced parents, we feel guilty and concerned about our future relationships with our children, what can we do? I think we need to be honest with them, as I tried to be with Jay and Grant. We need to let them know, even if they push us away, that we love them and that they matter deeply to us. We need to let them know, even if they bang shut the door, that we'll always be there if they need us and that while we understand how they feel now, we hope that their feelings will change. Above all, we need to make sure that we confront and deal with in ourselves the very human tendency to want to hurt them back—either by facing them in anger or by ignoring them. If we expect our children to come back to us, we somehow have to rise above the turmoil and act like . . . parents.

My greatest fear was that Jay and Grant would not recognize or, if they did, would not accept as real the enormous changes that had taken place in me since my divorce from their mother. The temptation was enormous to tell them: "Look, look how I'm different now. I'm no longer the angry father you once knew." But enormous changes can't be talked about; they have to be seen. I had to show by my behavior that I was different. And that took time, lots of time.

For a long while I felt terribly guilty that we no longer were a family. But I can see now, after these many years, that we are a family again. Yes, it's a different kind of family, separated by miles, lifestyles, and philosophies, but it's a family nonetheless.

A family, I believe, is love. And we have love.